DEDICATION

To my wife, Carolyn, for her unwavering love and support, from the very beginning and always. This book is hers as much as mine.

ACKNOWLEDGMENTS

Many people worked behind the scenes to make this book possible and words alone barely express my gratitude to all of them for their unswerving encouragement and support throughout the project.

I was privileged to work with and have the complete and dedicated support of an extremely talented team of professionals at MetroBooks. I am especially grateful to my editor, Sharyn Rosart, whose enthusiasm for the book and complete faith in me set the team's course for a successful journey through to final printed page. I am extremely indebted to Kevin Ullrich, art director, for his imaginative visual presentation

...we here highly resolve that these dead shall not have died in vain...

REMEMBER DEC. 7th!

of the book. Special thanks go to Chris Kincade and Nathaniel Marunas for their valuable suggestions and skills, which enriched my writing. Many thanks go also to Jamie Ruszkai, photo editor, and Richela Morgan, production manager, for their contributions.

I also owe a debt of gratitude to a special group of friends from whom I drew the courage and inspiration, not to mention the enthusiasm, to write this book. My sincere thanks to noted author Paul Stillwell of the Naval Institute for his recommendation. Thanks also to Pearl Harbor survivor and historian Robert A. Varrill and his wife, Ann, for the use of their book *The White Book of Pearl Harbor Data*.

For my daughter, Lee Anne Fernandez, and good friend Robert D. Bracci, a Pearl Harbor historian, a special heartfelt thank you, for their patience and advice. I wish also to thank Stan Cohen of Pictorial Histories, Bess Taubman of Mapmania Publishing, and John F. De Virgilio and David Aiken, both Directors of the Pearl Harbor History Associates, Inc., for their involvement and contributions of material.

Finally, a very gracious thank you to those who endeavor to keep the memory of Pearl Harbor alive and especially to the men and women who were present on Oahu on December 7th, 1941. "Remember Pearl Harbor!"

PEARL HARBOR

PEARL HARBOR

Ernest Arroyo

MetroBooks

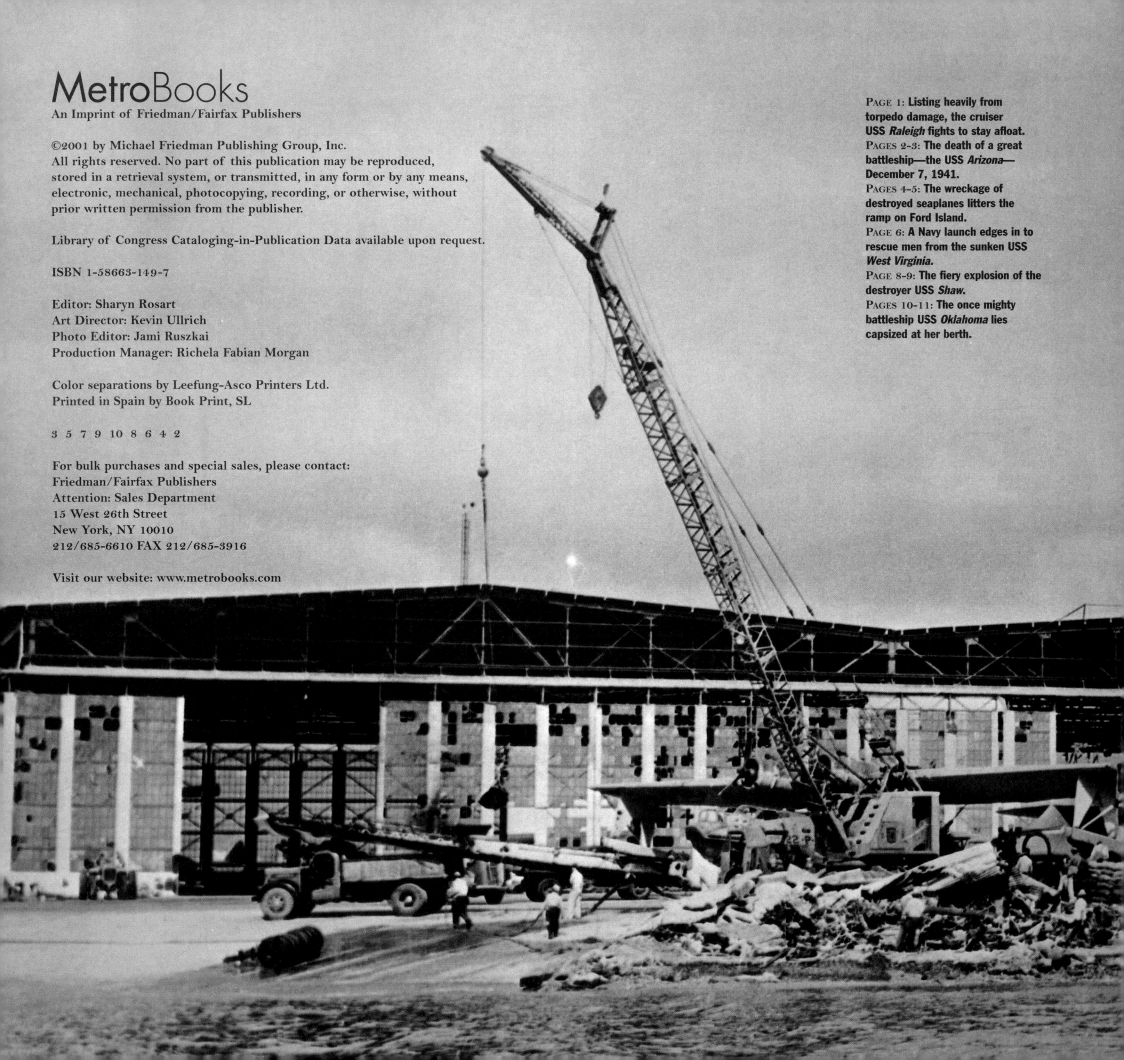

MetroBooks

An Imprint of Friedman/Fairfax Publishers

©2001 by Michael Friedman Publishing Group, Inc.

Library of Congress Cataloging-in-Publication Data available upon request.

ISBN 1-58663-149-7

Editor: Sharyn Rosart
Art Director: Kevin Ullrich
Photo Editor: Jami Ruszkai
Production Manager: Richela Fabian Morgan

Color separations by Leefung-Asco Printers Ltd.
Printed in Spain by Book Print, SL

3 5 7 9 10 8 6 4 2

For bulk purchases and special sales, please contact:
Friedman/Fairfax Publishers
Attention: Sales Department
15 West 26th Street
New York, NY 10010
212/685-6610 FAX 212/685-3916

Visit our website: www.metrobooks.com

PAGE 1: **Listing heavily from torpedo damage, the cruiser USS *Raleigh* fights to stay afloat.**
PAGES 2-3: **The death of a great battleship—the USS *Arizona*—December 7, 1941.**
PAGES 4-5: **The wreckage of destroyed seaplanes litters the ramp on Ford Island.**
PAGE 6: **A Navy launch edges in to rescue men from the sunken USS *West Virginia*.**
PAGE 8-9: **The fiery explosion of the destroyer USS *Shaw*.**
PAGES 10-11: **The once mighty battleship USS *Oklahoma* lies capsized at her berth.**

Contents

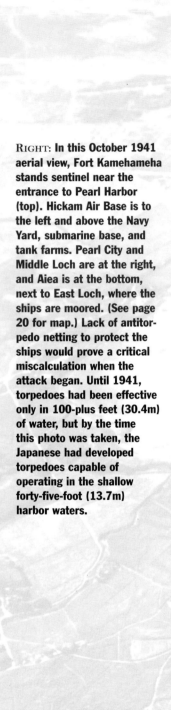

THE ROAD TO INFAMY

RIGHT: **In this October 1941
aerial view, Fort Kamehameha
stands sentinel near the
entrance to Pearl Harbor
(top). Hickam Air Base is to
the left and above the Navy
Yard, submarine base, and
tank farms. Pearl City and
Middle Loch are at the right,
and Aiea is at the bottom,
next to East Loch, where the
ships are moored. (See page
20 for map.) Lack of antitor-
pedo netting to protect the
ships would prove a critical
miscalculation when the
attack began. Until 1941,
torpedoes had been effective
only in 100-plus feet (30.4m)
of water, but by the time
this photo was taken, the
Japanese had developed
torpedoes capable of
operating in the shallow
forty-five-foot (13.7m)
harbor waters.**

Japan's expansionist intentions became clear in September 1931, when after a manufactured incident at a railway terminal on the Korean border, the Japanese Army invaded Manchuria and established a puppet regime, renaming it Manchuko. When the League of Nations condemned this action, the Japanese government withdrew from the League. Six years later, in July 1937, Japan launched a full-scale invasion of China. Though they were unable to move far into mainland China, by 1939, the Japanese troops had taken the coastal ports. The United States, which was committed to China's independence and was wary of Japan's imperialist ambitions, responded by stopping the export of strategic materials to Japan. Deprived of these materials, Japan turned its gaze to the riches of the East Indies and Southeast Asia, resources that would help build a self-sufficient empire.

In April 1940, as a deterrent to Japan's ambitions in the Far East, President Franklin D. Roosevelt ordered the U.S. Pacific Fleet to be moved permanently from the California coast to Hawaii's Pearl Harbor, on the island of Oahu. Relations between the United States and Japan, already in decline, worsened in September 1940, when Japan signed the Tripartite Pact with Nazi Germany and Fascist Italy. The situation had deteriorated further by April 1941, when Japan signed a non-aggression pact with the USSR.

In the months that followed, the United States and Japan engaged in numerous diplomatic exchanges but were unable to come to terms that were acceptable to both sides. When Japan forced the Vichy government to cede its holdings in French Indochina in July 1941, Roosevelt responded by placing an embargo on the sale of petroleum to Japan and by freezing all Japanese assets in the United States. Japan imported nearly 80 percent of its crucially needed oil from the United States; the embargo strengthened the Japanese resolve to secure access to the resources it needed without having to rely on the United States.

Recognizing that neither the United States nor Great Britain was fully ready for war in the Pacific, Japan prepared to seize the initiative, planning a rapid strike to take the so-called Southern regions. On September 6, 1941 the Japanese High Command concluded that there was no alternative but to set in motion the Southern Operation plan for the conquest of Southeast Asia.

LEFT: **Men of Company C, 11th Field Artillery, 24th Infantry Division, Schofield Barracks pose outside their post at Battery C.**
BELOW: **Surprisingly, on the night of December 6, many at Schofield remained at their posts. Corporal Joseph S. Rutkowski (right, with a buddy) watched the movie** *Honky Tonk*, **starring Clark Gable and Jean Harlow, at the post theater. After a few beers at the post PX, Corporal Rutkowski spent the rest of the evening writing home.**

LEFT: **During peacetime, most servicemen considered the Hawaiian Islands a good tour of duty and a new adventure. When off duty, most soldiers and sailors would head for the YMCA, a convenient meeting place, or enjoy a quick beer and bite to eat at the Black Cat Cafe across the street. From there, they could fan out on the town. Some would take in the taverns at Waikiki Beach, while most went down to Hotel Street, a hodgepodge of arcades, tattoo joints, souvenir shops, and such bars as Two Jacks, Emma's New Café, or the Mint. Bawdy hotels like the New Senators, the Rex, or the Anchor Hotel were also options. Here, a group of servicemen enjoy a traditional hula presentation.**

RIGHT: **Pictured here six weeks before the attack, the submarine base, fuel storage tanks, and ship-repair facilities would have been prime targets had the Japanese raiders returned for a third strike; instead, the structures survived the nearly two-hour attack undamaged. Loss of these vital facilities would have been a crippling blow, forcing the U.S. fleet to return operations to the West Coast. Vice Admiral Chuichi Nagumo, unaware of the location of the U.S. carriers, decided against the third attack wave. He felt his mission, the destruction of the U.S. Battle Fleet, had been accomplished.**

LIEUTENANT GENERAL WALTER C. SHORT
United States Army

Born in Fillmore, Illinois, on March 30, 1880, Lieutenant General Short served in the army for nearly forty years, a classic example of a fine infantry officer rising through the ranks. On February 7, 1941, he assumed command of the U.S. Army's Hawaiian Department. His threefold mission was the coastal defense of Hawaii, the training of new arrivals, and the protection of the Pacific Fleet when it was in Pearl Harbor. On the evening of December 6, 1941, Lieutenant General and Mrs. Short and their guests left the Schofield Officers' Club for the drive to Fort Shafter. As the road sloped down, they could see the lights of the harbor spreading out in the distance. "Isn't that a beautiful sight?" Short sighed, before adding, prophetically, "And what a target it would make."

Short and his friend and navy counterpart Admiral Husband Edward Kimmel would be held responsible for the Pearl Harbor disaster, charged with "dereliction of duty" and errors in judgment. Short, who requested but was never granted a court-martial, retired in 1942; later, the charges against him were dropped.

General Short remains an enigma. Though exonerated, he wrote no books, left no personal papers or diaries, and never spoke about the event. His dignified silence was that of a career army man whose conscience was clear. Short died on September 3, 1949.

LEFT: In 1940, the Pacific Fleet, seen here in the distance off the coast of downtown Honolulu, was moved to Hawaii to deter Japanese ambitions in the Far East. Admiral James O. Richardson, then Commander in Chief, U.S. Pacific Fleet, opposed the move, believing the fleet would be too removed from the logistical and industrial support of the U.S. West Coast. He was eventually relieved of his command by President Franklin D. Roosevelt and replaced by Admiral H.E. Kimmel. The fleet was in the Islands to stay.

ABOVE: Admiral H.E. Kimmel (center), Commander in Chief, Pacific Fleet in 1941, discusses the Far East situation over a map with his operations officer, Captain Walter S. DeLany (left), and his chief of staff, Captain William W. Smith. On December 2, Kimmel's intelligence officer, Lieutenant Commander Edwin T. Layton, informed him that there had been no Japanese radio communications regarding the whereabouts of the Imperial Navy's Carrier Divisions One and Two. Kimmel smiled and said, jokingly, "You don't know where they are? Do you mean to say that they could be rounding Diamond Head and you wouldn't know it?" Layton answered abjectly, "I hope they would be sighted by now, sir."

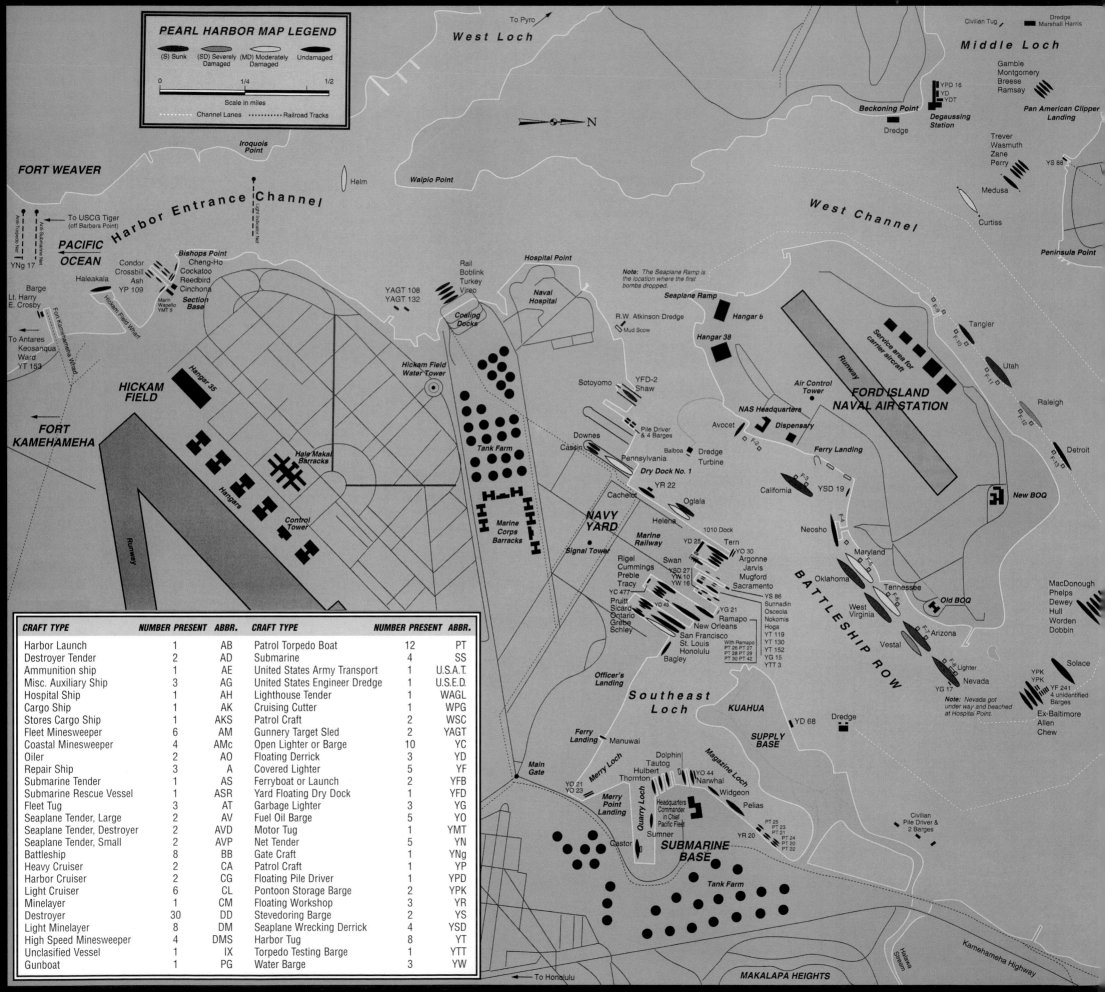

PEARL HARBOR MAP LEGEND

(S) Sunk   (SD) Severely Damaged   (MD) Moderately Damaged   Undamaged

Scale in miles

0   1/4   1/2

········· Channel Lanes   ········· Railroad Tracks

West Loch

To Pyro

Middle Loch

Civilian Tug   Dredge Marshall Harris

Beckoning Point

Degaussing Station

YPD 16
YD
YDT

Dredge

Pan American Clipper Landing

Gamble
Montgomery
Breese
Ramsay

Trever
Wasmuth
Zane
Perry

YS 88

Medusa

Curtiss

West Channel

Peninsula Point

Iroquois Point

FORT WEAVER

Helm

Waipio Point

Harbor Entrance Channel

Light Indicator Net

To USCG Tiger (off Barbers Point)

PACIFIC OCEAN

Anti-Torpedo Net
Anti-Submarine Net
YNg 17

Haleakala

Fort Kamehameha Wharf

Hickam Field Wharf

Condor
Crossbill
Ash   YP 109

Bishops Point
Cheng-Ho
Cockatoo
Reedbird
Cinchona

Marin
Wapello
YMT 5

Section Base

Barge
Lt. Harry
E. Crosby

To Antares
Keosanqua
Ward
YT 153

HICKAM FIELD

Hangar 35

FORT KAMEHAMEHA

Runway

Hangars

Control Tower

Hale Makai Barracks

YAGT 108
YAGT 132

Rail
Boblink
Turkey
Vireo

Coaling Docks

Hickam Field Water Tower

Tank Farm

Marine Corps Barracks

Hospital Point

Naval Hospital

Note: The Seaplane Ramp is the location where the first bombs dropped.

Seaplane Ramp

R.W. Atkinson Dredge

Mud Scow

Hangar 6

Hangar 38

FORD ISLAND NAVAL AIR STATION

Service area for carrier aircraft

Runway

Tangier

Utah

Raleigh

Detroit

Sotoyomo

YFD-2
Shaw

Downes

Cassin

Pennsylvania

Dry Dock No. 1

YR 22

Cachelot

NAVY YARD

Signal Tower

Oglala

Helena

Balboa
Dredge Turbine

Pile Driver & 4 Barges

NAS Headquarters

Avocet

California

Neosho

Maryland

Oklahoma

West Virginia

Tennessee

Arizona

Vestal

Air Control Tower

Dispensary

Ferry Landing

YSD 19

F-3

F-5

F-6

F-7

F-8 Lighter

New BOQ

Old BOQ

BATTLESHIP ROW

MacDonald
Phelps
Dewey
Hull
Worden
Dobbin

Marine Railway

Rigel
Cummings
Preble
Tracy
YC 477
Pruitt
Sicard
Ontario
Grebe
Schley

1010 Dock

YD 25

Swan

YSD 27
YW 10
YW 16

YO 43

Tern

YO 30
Argonne
Jarvis
Mugford
Sacramento

YS 86
Sunnadin
Osceola
Nokomis
Hoga

New Orleans

San Francisco
St. Louis
Honolulu
Bagley

Ramapo
YG 21

YT 119
YT 130
YT 152
YG 15
YTT 3

With Ramapo
PT 26 PT 27
PT 28 PT 29
PT 30 PT 42

Nevada

YG 17

Solace

YPK
YPK
YF 241
4 unidentified Barges

Ex-Baltimore
Allen
Chew

Note: Nevada got under way and beached at Hospital Point.

Officer's Landing

Southeast Loch

KUAHUA

YD 68

Dredge

SUPPLY BASE

Main Gate

Ferry Landing

Manuwai

Merry Loch

Merry Point Landing

YO 21
YO 23

Merry Loch

Quarry Loch

Headquarters Commander in Chief Pacific Fleet

Sumner

Castor

Dolphin
Tautog
Hulbert
Thornton

YO 44
Narwhal

Widgeon

Pelias

Magazine Loch

SUBMARINE BASE

Tank Farm

YR 20

PT 25 PT 23
PT 21
PT 24
PT 20
PT 22

Civilian Pile Driver & 2 Barges

To Honolulu

MAKALAPA HEIGHTS

Halawa Stream

Kamehameha Highway

CRAFT TYPE	NUMBER PRESENT	ABBR.	CRAFT TYPE	NUMBER PRESENT	ABBR.
Harbor Launch	1	AB	Patrol Torpedo Boat	12	PT
Destroyer Tender	2	AD	Submarine	4	SS
Ammunition ship	1	AE	United States Army Transport	1	U.S.A.T.
Misc. Auxiliary Ship	3	AG	United States Engineer Dredge	1	U.S.E.D.
Hospital Ship	1	AH	Lighthouse Tender	1	WAGL
Cargo Ship	1	AK	Cruising Cutter	1	WPG
Stores Cargo Ship	1	AKS	Patrol Craft	2	WSC
Fleet Minesweeper	6	AM	Gunnery Target Sled	2	YAGT
Coastal Minesweeper	4	AMc	Open Lighter or Barge	10	YC
Oiler	2	AO	Floating Derrick	3	YD
Repair Ship	3	A	Covered Lighter	5	YF
Submarine Tender	1	AS	Ferryboat or Launch	2	YFB
Submarine Rescue Vessel	1	ASR	Yard Floating Dry Dock	1	YFD
Fleet Tug	3	AT	Garbage Lighter	3	YG
Seaplane Tender, Large	2	AV	Fuel Oil Barge	5	YO
Seaplane Tender, Destroyer	2	AVD	Motor Tug	1	YMT
Seaplane Tender, Small	2	AVP	Net Tender	5	YN
Battleship	8	BB	Gate Craft	1	YNg
Heavy Cruiser	2	CA	Patrol Craft	1	YP
Harbor Cruiser	2	CG	Floating Pile Driver	1	YPD
Light Cruiser	6	CL	Pontoon Storage Barge	2	YPK
Minelayer	1	CM	Floating Workshop	3	YR
Destroyer	30	DD	Stevedoring Barge	2	YS
Light Minelayer	8	DM	Seaplane Wrecking Derrick	4	YSD
High Speed Minesweeper	4	DMS	Harbor Tug	8	YT
Unclasified Vessel	1	IX	Torpedo Testing Barge	1	YTT
Gunboat	1	PG	Water Barge	3	YW

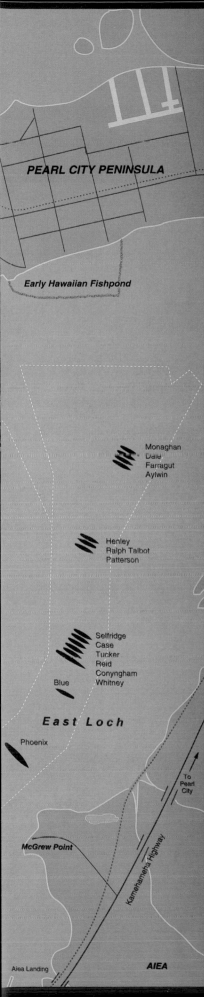

PEARL CITY PENINSULA

Early Hawaiian Fishpond

Monaghan
Dale
Farragut
Aylwin

Henley
Ralph Talbot
Patterson

Selfridge
Case
Tucker
Reid
Conyngham
Blue   Whitney

East Loch

Phoenix

To
Pearl
City

McGrew Point

Kamehameha Highway

Aiea Landing   AIEA

LEFT: At the time of the attack, nearly half the U.S. Pacific Fleet was in Pearl Harbor, a group that included battleships, cruisers, destroyers, and submarines. Other types of naval vessels also in port included repair ships, tenders, various minecraft, oilers, store ships, tugboats, and one hospital ship. This map shows the position of each ship on the morning of December 7, as well as the location of important facilities and landmarks.

ABOVE: Taken six weeks before the attack, this photo shows Ford Island Naval Air Station to the left and the Pearl Harbor Navy Yard in the center, next to the sprawling U.S. Army Air Force Base, Hickam Field. In this view, two destroyers can be seen passing through the open antisubmarine nets spanning the main channel. On the morning of December 7, the nets were opened to allow a navy cargo ship, the USS *Antares*, to enter the harbor; as the attack began, a Japanese midget sub managed to sneak through.

PLAN Z—THE HAWAII OPERATION

RIGHT: **An A6M2 Zero fighter plane, armed with two wing-mounted 20mm cannons and two 7.7mm machine guns in the engine cowling, prepares to launch from the flight deck of the Japanese carrier *Shokaku* ("Soaring Crane"). B5N2 Nakajima high-level bombers warm up behind it. These were among the 167 planes of the second attack wave; no known photographs exist of the first wave's launch at 0600. As soon as it was ready, the second wave lined up in the early morning light. Every flying officer and crewman wore a white scarf, called a *hachimaki*—traditionally a symbol for courage and determination—around his head.**

The attack on Pearl Harbor was not undertaken as a singular operation, but as part of Japan's larger plan for the conquest of Southeast Asia. The primary objective was to secure the much-coveted oil, rubber, tin, and other natural resources that had been denied them by economic sanctions. Without these resources, Japan's industry would be crippled and the military would be prevented from operating as an offensive force. France, Holland, and Belgium had already fallen before the German Blitzkrieg, while England was on the defensive. Realizing that the European nations could no longer defend their colonial possessions, Japan realized that the time was right to put the Southern Operation plan in motion.

Admiral Isoroku Yamamoto did not want to wage war against the United States. But if Japan was going to launch such a war, he believed they should strike the first blow and strike hard. He was convinced that a surprise air attack by naval aircraft to try to wipe out the U.S. fleet at Pearl Harbor—followed by swift occupation of Borneo, Java, Singapore, Sumatra, and the Philippines—would, if successful, leave America sufficiently demoralized to accept a negotiated peace. This was the only way to prevent the Americans from obstructing Japan's plans for Southeast Asia.

Commander Minoru Genda, a brilliant aerial tactician and experienced carrier pilot, was charged with turning Yamamoto's idea into a working plan. Genda concluded that such an attack would be difficult, but not impossible. The plan required the coordination of carriers, destroyers, cruisers, and battleships, along with high-level bombers, dive-bombers, and fighters. Yamamoto named the plan Operation Z (after Admiral Togo's famous "Z" signal made on the eve of the Russo-Japanese War's Battle of Tsushima in 1905). On November 26, 1941 the forces, having gathered secretly in the Kuril Islands over the preceding weeks, sailed for Hawaii.

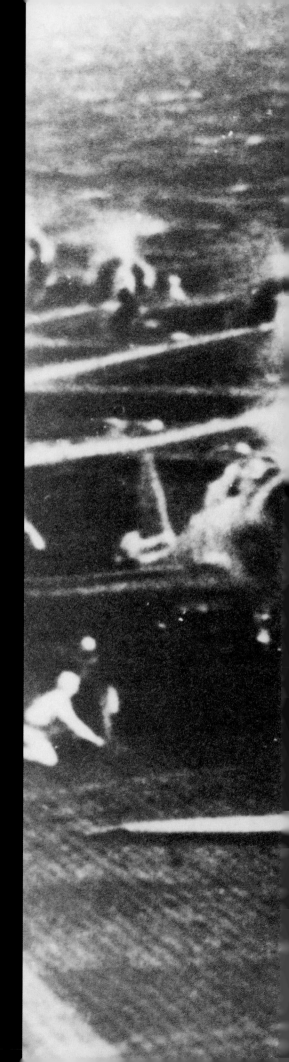

LEFT: **The carrier USS *Saratoga* (foreground) and her sister ship, the USS *Lexington*, sit peacefully at anchor off Diamond Head. Carriers were the prime targets of the Japanese raiders, but not one was in port during the attack. The *Lexington* had departed Pearl Harbor on December 5 with Task Group 12 to deliver eighteen scout bombers to Midway Island, and the *Saratoga* was undergoing a general overhaul at Puget Sound Navy Yard on the West Coast of the United States. Another carrier away from port during the attack, the USS *Enterprise*, was returning on December 7 after delivering F4F-3 Wildcat fighter planes to Wake Island. About 250 miles (400km) due west of Oahu, she launched eighteen SBD Dauntless scout planes to patrol 150 miles (240km) ahead of the task force and then fly on to Ford Island Naval Air Station. The pilots were unaware they were flying into the middle of the Japanese onslaught. Only twelve of the eighteen planes landed safely. The others were shot down.**

RIGHT: **Emperor Hirohito, "The Voice of the Crane" (first row, right), is pictured here with his cabinet in a photo that probably was taken in the late 1930s. According to tradition, the emperor was the Son of Heaven and a direct descendent of the sun goddess, Amaterasu. War Minister Hideki Tojo (second row, second from left) became the prime minister in July 1941 and led his country into war with America.**

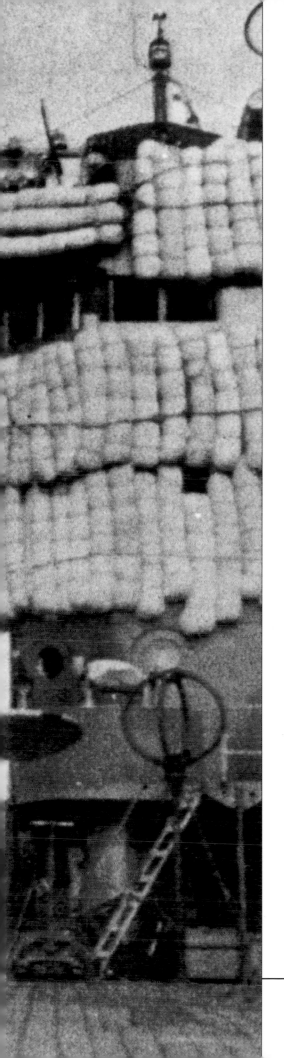

LEFT: Having gathered secretly in Hitokappu Bay, in Japan's bleak northern Kuril Islands, the strike force sailed on November 26 with thirty-one ships, bound for Pearl Harbor.

BELOW: The carrier *Akagi* was the flagship of Admiral Chuichi Nagumo, whose First Air Fleet consisted of six of Japan's finest aircraft carriers. Nagumo's assigned mission was to "advance into Hawaiian waters, and at the very opening of hostilities, attack the main force of the U.S. Fleet in Hawaii." At 855 feet (259.9m) long, the *Akagi* displaced 36,500 tons (33,105.5t), had a top speed of 31 knots, and carried ninety-one planes.

LEFT: The Japanese strike force, under strict radio silence, had chosen to sail the lesser-used northern passage across the Pacific to its objective. Stormy seas, gales, and thick fog along this route contributed to its good luck avoiding detection. The day before the attack, as the crew is being briefed, Petty Officer First Class Tadeo Kimura's A6M2 Zero fighter stands on the deck of the *Akagi* ("Red Castle"). An unusual bomb-splinter padding, made up of rolled-up mattresses, can be seen on the bridge of the ship's island.

RIGHT: **As part of the precision attack waves, a high-level bomber lifts off from the carrier *Shokaku* on December 7. Once the strike force reached its launch point 230 miles (368km) north of Oahu, it took only fifteen minutes in the predawn darkness to get the first wave's 183 aircraft into the sky.**

U.S. servicemen had difficulty remembering the numbering system for Japanese aircraft. To make identification and communications easier in the heat of battle, U.S. Army Intelligence devised a system whereby simple English names were assigned to each type of plane. Thus, the D3A1 dive-bomber was dubbed the "Val," the A6M2 Zero was the "Zeke," and the B5N2 Nakajima bomber was named "Kate."

ABOVE: Pictured here, the *Hiryu* ("Flying Dragon") was 746 feet (226.8m) long, had a complement of seventy-three aircraft, and (like the rest of the fleet) ferried many anxious Japanese servicemen to their first combat missions. On the twelve-day journey to the launch point, the men found different ways to calm their nerves. Aboard the *Hiryu's* sister carrier, the *Soryu* ("Green Dragon"), Lieutenant Iyozo Fujita drank a few bottles of beer and then took a hot bath the night before the attack. He wished to go into battle fresh and clean, as had the Samurai warriors of old.

LEFT: In the early morning light, a flight crew lines the deck of the carrier *Zuikaku* ("Happy Crane") as a B5N2 Nakajima "Kate" bomber prepares for takeoff. One hour after the first wave had departed, the second attack wave lifted off. Flight crews sent them off with shouts of encouragement and yells of "Banzai! Banzai!" and "Long live the Emperor!"

ADMIRAL ISOROKU YAMAMOTO, COMMANDER IN CHIEF
Japanese Combined Fleet

The son of a schoolmaster, Isoroku Yamamoto graduated from the Japanese naval academy at Eta Jima in 1904. After World War I, he studied at Harvard University, and in 1925 was sent to Washington, D.C., for a tour of duty as naval attaché. Largely responsible for the development of Japan's naval aviation program, Yamamoto was a great motivator and complex person. He loved games of chance, but did not smoke or drink; he was a bible reader, but not a Christian; and he had a sense of humor, but was reserved and very calm in demeanor. Outspoken in his opposition to war with the United States.

Yamamoto knew Japan was no match for the industrial might of the Americans. "If I am told to fight," he said, "regardless of the consequences, I shall run wild for the first six months or a year, but I have utterly no confidence for the second or third year." Yamamoto was killed on April 18, 1943, while on an inspection tour of Japanese bases in the Solomon Islands, when his plane was shot down. His ashes were returned to Tokyo, where he was given a state funeral (only the second one ever accorded to a commoner in Japanese history).

ABOVE: On the morning of December 7, as the planes were being readied, the pilots and crews were inspired by patriotic words from officers and comrades. Captain Koji Shiroshime, commanding officer of the carrier *Shokaku*, stands before a blackboard that reads: "Japanese Imperial Fleet! You must obey and die for your country, Japan! Whether you win or lose, you must fight and die for your country!" As the first wave of planes neared Barber's Point on Oahu, Lieutenant Commander Mitsuo Fuchida, chosen to lead the first wave of the attack, radioed back to the carriers: "Tora! Tora! Tora!" ("Tiger! Tiger! Tiger!") The now famous code words meant the Japanese had caught the U.S. fleet completely by surprise. Incredibly, the signal was heard on Admiral Yamamoto's flagship, the *Nagato*, at anchor in Japan's Inland Sea.

BELOW: **On December 7, with the attack already underway for an hour, Ambassador Kichisaburo Nomura (far left) and Special Envoy Saburo Kuruso (with hat) leave the U.S. State Department. The diplomats, who would not learn of the attack until they returned to their embassy, had just presented Secretary of State Cordell Hull with Tokyo's final note ending negotiations. Hull, who already knew about the attack, had excused the two very curtly. Hull was aware of the attack because U.S. intelligence's "Magic" operation had cracked the Japanese diplomatic code, J-19 (a.k.a. "Purple"). Washington, however, had overlooked the critical meaning of some of the decrypted messages; more importantly, there had been no mention of Japanese military intentions in any of the diplomatic messages.**

Admiral Husband E. Kimmel
United States Navy

With a warm Hawaiian sun beaming down on the quarterdeck, Admiral H.E. Kimmel "broke his flag"(the expression refers to the part of the change-of-command ceremony during which the previous admiral's flag is taken down and the new one's raised) on February 1, 1941, at the main truck (flagstaff) of the battleship *Pennsylvania*. Kimmel was appointed by President Roosevelt in relief of Admiral Richardson as Commander in Chief, U.S. Pacific Fleet. A graduate of the Naval Academy Class of 1904, Kimmel had a distinguished career of naval service and had earned a reputation as a highly capable officer.

Kimmel saw to it that his new command was prepared for warfare, should war come, by ensuring that the ships were battle-ready and the men were well trained and in a high state of readi- ness. Due to the success of the Japanese surprise attack, however, Kimmel received much of the blame for the naval forces' poor response. At his headquarters during the raid, he was standing by a window when a spent bullet smashed through the glass and hit him lightly in the chest. He picked up the bullet and said to an aide, "It would have been merciful had it killed me." He retired in 1942 and was later cleared of most charges by a postwar Congressional inquiry.

CHAPTER TWO

"AIR RAID PEARL HARBOR. THIS IS NOT A DRILL!"

RIGHT: White smoke rises from the burning hangars and planes on the flight line at Hickam Field. Seen in the water are shock waves from previous explosions and the wakes from torpedoes streaking towards Battleship Row. Ahead of the USS *Nevada*, lower left, the USS *Vestal*, a repair ship (her movie screen still up from the night before) is tied up outboard of the USS *Arizona*, these ships have not yet been hit. The wakes of two more torpedoes head for the USS *West Virginia*, already listing to port and leaking fuel oil from previous strikes. The USS *Tennessee* lies inboard and undamaged. The USS *Maryland*, also undamaged, is tied up inboard of the USS *Oklahoma*, which is taking on water and beginning to list. The tanker USS *Neosho*, undamaged, is at the gasoline pier, while the USS *California*, ahead of her, spills fuel oil into the harbor after a torpedo strike. At Ten-Ten Dock (center), the cruiser USS *Helena* spews smoke from another torpedo hit.

At 0900 in Washington, D.C. (0330 A.M. Hawaii time), on the morning of the attack, a Japanese diplomatic message was intercepted and decoded. Representatives of the Japanese embassy planned to meet with U.S. Secretary of State Cordell Hull at 1300 (0730 in Hawaii), to officially announce Japan's intent to break off negotiations. In response, General George C. Marshall radioed Hawaii, Panama, and the Philippines with the following message: "The Japanese are presenting today at 1:00 P.M. what amounts to an ultimatum. Just what significance the hour set may have we do not know, but be on the alert accordingly." Due to atmospheric difficulties in the Pacific, however, the message for Hawaii, which was not marked urgent, was sent via Western Union at 12:17 P.M., Washington time. General Short was to receive it five hours after the attack had ended.

Meanwhile, it was early Sunday morning on Oahu. The early risers who heard planes overhead assumed they were part of U.S. Army or Navy maneuvers. At Kaneohe Naval Air Station, the post medical officer, Lieutenant Commander H.P. McCrimmon, was at his office wondering, as many others would that morning, why the Sunday paper hadn't been delivered yet. He looked out the window and saw three planes flying in close formation at tree-top height, firing machine guns. It wasn't until black smoke and flames began erupting from the parked planes and hangars that McCrimmon realized what was happening.

At 0755 Lieutenant Commander Logan Ramsey was on duty in Ford Island's control center when he heard the unmistakable sound of a diving plane, followed by a blast at the hangar area. Realizing what had happened, he immediately broadcast the message: "Air raid Pearl Harbor. This is not drill!" and ordered all radiomen on duty to send out the news: the time was 0758. The message flew out from ships and stations: "Enemy air raid. No drill!" and "Air raid Pearl Harbor. This is not a drill!" as explosions shook the harbor.

RIGHT: A two-man midget submarine washes ashore off Bellows Field. The Japanese Imperial Navy planned on using five of these eighty-one-by-six-foot (24.3X1.8m) subs, each armed with two 18-inch (45.7cm) torpedoes. The subs were ferried to Pearl Harbor on the decks of large fleet submarines and deployed at midnight on December 6, ten miles (16km) from the harbor. Only one midget entered the harbor successfully; it was detected and sunk before damaging any U.S. ships. Another was sunk an hour before the attack, this one was captured on December 8, and still another was found in 1960, its torpedoes intact. The whereabouts of the fifth remains a mystery to this day.

LEFT: This Japanese chart of Pearl Harbor was found in the sub on the opposite page; it shows the anchorage of major warships, plus an apparent attack and escape route. The map was most likely compiled from information provided by undercover agent Ensign Takeo Yoshikawa, who worked out of the Japanese Consulate in Honolulu. Yoshikawa provided information to the Japanese Navy on U.S. ship movements, harbor defenses, air patrol schedules, ships' berthing plans, and if torpedo netting was being used. Placed under house arrest after the attack, Yoshikawa was later sent back to Japan in an exchange of diplomatic prisoners. The United States did not learn of his spy activities until years after the war.

ABOVE: At 0645 on December 7, an unidentified submarine was spotted off the harbor entrance, apparently trying to sneak into the harbor behind an incoming supply ship. Lieutenant William Outerbridge, commanding the destroyer USS *Ward* (above), gave the order, "General quarters," summoning all hands to their battle stations, and the ship sprang into action. He reported to headquarters: "We have attacked, fired upon and dropped depth charges upon unidentified submarine operating in defensive sea area." The *Ward* had fired the first shots of the war for the United States. Before the rest of the navy could react fully, though, the air raid had begun.

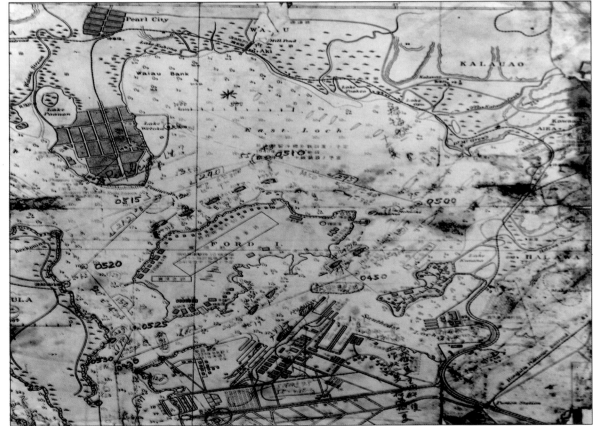

ABOVE: The Sunday morning of the attack found the USS *Solace*, a converted passenger liner newly commissioned as a hospital ship, moored in East Loch, off Ford Island. The medical staff was in the midst of its rounds and the crew was preparing the ship for religious services when the tranquility was shattered by the explosions on Battleship Row. Casualties soon began to arrive at the hospital ship, ferried by many small boats. The ship's staff and crew members tended to the hundreds of dying and wounded throughout the day and night. For the heroic work of the ship's staff and crew, the *Solace* was awarded the Navy Unit Citation; it was the only hospital ship to receive the award in World War II.

ABOVE: To detect aircraft like the Japanese Aichi D3A1 dive-bomber seen here, the U.S. Army relied on five brand-new SCR-270-B mobile radar units. With few or no spare parts, the radar devices were operated from 0400 to 0700, the time of day when General Short believed the Island most vulnerable to air attack. On the morning of December 7, two privates, Joseph L. Lockard and George E. Elliott, stayed on the air late for extra training at the Opana Mobile Radar Station. Picking up a contact of planes bigger then anything they had seen before, they reported it to headquarters at Fort Shafter and were told it was most likely a flight of twelve B-17s due in from California. In fact, it was the Japanese air armada approaching Oahu. New in 1941, radar technology could not distinguish the number of planes, their altitude, or whether they were friend or foe.

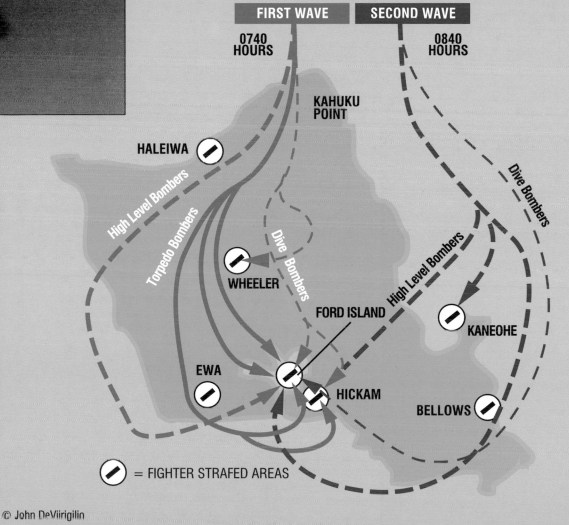

FIRST WAVE SECOND WAVE

0740 HOURS 0840 HOURS

KAHUKU POINT

HALEIWA

High Level Bombers

Torpedo Bombers

Dive Bombers

Dive Bombers

WHEELER

High Level Bombers

FORD ISLAND

KANEOHE

EWA

HICKAM

BELLOWS

= FIGHTER STRAFED AREAS

© John DeViirigilin

"AIR RAID PEARL HARBOR. THIS IS NOT A DRILL!"

ABOVE: **Nearly five minutes before the attack on Battleship Row, a B5N2 Nakajima bomber soars over the devastation of burning hangars and seaplanes at Kaneohe Bay. In December 1941, Kaneohe Naval Air Station was Oahu's newest military installation. Though construction was still in progress, it was an operational base and home to Patrol Wing One and its thirty-six PBY-5 Catalina seaplanes. The base was targeted by the Japanese first to prevent the patrol planes from searching for the strike force. In the first attack wave, a flight of eleven Japanese Zeros swooped down from the north to strafe the seaplane base with incendiary bullets fired from the planes' machine guns and cannons.**

RIGHT: **At the Kaneohe Bachelors' Officers Quarters when the strike began, five pilots jumped into Ensign Charles Willis' car and sped off to the hangar area. Surviving intense strafing en route, the men got out of the car just as a bullet detonated the gas tank. The destruction of the car was nothing compared to the holocaust around them, with black smoke and flames erupting from the planes and hangars.**

ORDNANCEMAN JOHN WILLIAM FINN
United States Navy

During the attack on Kaneohe Bay, Chief Aviation Ordnanceman John William Finn was one of the first people on the ground to return fire, manning a .50 caliber anti-aircraft gun normally used for instruction. The gun's position, in a completely exposed section of the parking ramp near several seaplanes, left him open to heavy machine-gun fire as the Japanese planes strafed the area. His Medal of Honor citation, "for extraordinary heroism, distinguished service, and devotion above and "beyond the call of duty," describes Finn's disregard for his own safety: "Although painfully wounded many times, he continued...to return the enemy's fire vigorously and with telling effect throughout the enemy strafing and bombing attacks.... It was only by specific orders that he was persuaded to leave his post to seek medical attention. Following first-aid treatment, although obviously suffering much pain and moving with great difficulty, he returned to the squadron area and actively supervised the rearming of returning planes. His extraordinary heroism and conduct in this action were in keeping with the highest traditions of the U.S. Naval Service."

Born in Los Angeles on July 24, 1909, Finn served in the U.S. Navy for twenty years, mustering out as a lieutenant in September 1946. At this writing, he remains the last living recipient of the fifteen Medals of Honor awarded during the Pearl Harbor attack.

ABOVE: Once the first group of Japanese Zeros flew off, men sprinted from cover to see what could be saved, some crying at the sight of their burning planes. One bullet-riddled plane was pushed to relative safety between two buildings, while this one, with its wing burning, was pushed into the bay to quench the flames. As the men undertook their salvage efforts, Chief Machinist Woodrow Wilson Beard saw a flight of horizontal bombers coming from seaward. "Take cover!" he yelled to the men. "Here comes the heavy stuff!"

RIGHT: Debris from the exploding bombs set more aircraft ablaze and completed the destruction of the two new hangars. A direct hit on Hangar One destroyed four PBY seaplanes inside, killing and wounding a number of men. As bullets ricocheted off the hangar walls, sailors, marines, and construction workers continued fighting the fires with complete disregard for their own safety.

ABOVE: With the Kaneohe Naval Air Station fire truck wrecked early in the attack, base personnel undertook Herculean fire-fighting efforts; salvage was understandably difficult during the onslaught. Since the base had no air defenses, rifles and Browning Automatic Rifles (BARs) were handed out, while the .50-caliber machine guns and ammunition from destroyed aircraft were set up as temporary anti-aircraft emplacements. Servicemen raced to save what they could.

Ensign Cecil S. Malwein recalled trying, with two other men, to move a plane with a tractor when another round of Japanese strafing set it on fire. The bombers then took care of everything the Zeros had missed. Thirty-three of Patrol Wing One's thirty-six PBYs were destroyed on the ramps, in the water, or in the hangars; the three surviving Catalina aircraft were on patrol at the time and returned after dark. All told, the Japanese inflicted seventeen fatalities, including two civilian construction workers, and wounded sixty-seven during the attack at Kaneohe.

ABOVE: Since Sunday was the one day they could sleep in, most of the men in the 72nd Pursuit Squadron at Wheeler Field were still in their tents when the Japanese struck. Private Wilfred J. Burk, however, was already up preparing for church services; when the bombs started exploding, he raced to the hangars to help save the aircraft. When he returned after the attack, the tent area had been bombed and strafed terribly. Upon reaching the spot where his tent had been, he was horrified by the devastation, some of which can be seen here—many of the 72nd's tents had been incinerated and the bodies of some of his friends lay in the ruins. A corporal then ordered him to help move the wounded to the dispensary.

RIGHT: A thick pall of black smoke hangs over the burning hangars and planes at Wheeler Field, home of the U.S. Army Air Force pursuit squadrons. Located next to Schofield Barracks in the center of Oahu, Wheeler came under attack at 0751. Twenty-five "Val" dive-bombers from the *Zuikaku* and eight Zeros from the *Soryu* bombed and strafed the airfield for fifteen minutes, destroying fifty-two aircraft, killing thirty-four men, and wounding fifty-three. To guard against possible sabotage, the planes had been parked in neat rows, wingtip to wingtip, and their ammunition stored in the hangars. Sergeant Mobley L. Hall, a crew chief, recalled that no instructions had been issued concerning an air attack, only against possible sabotage.

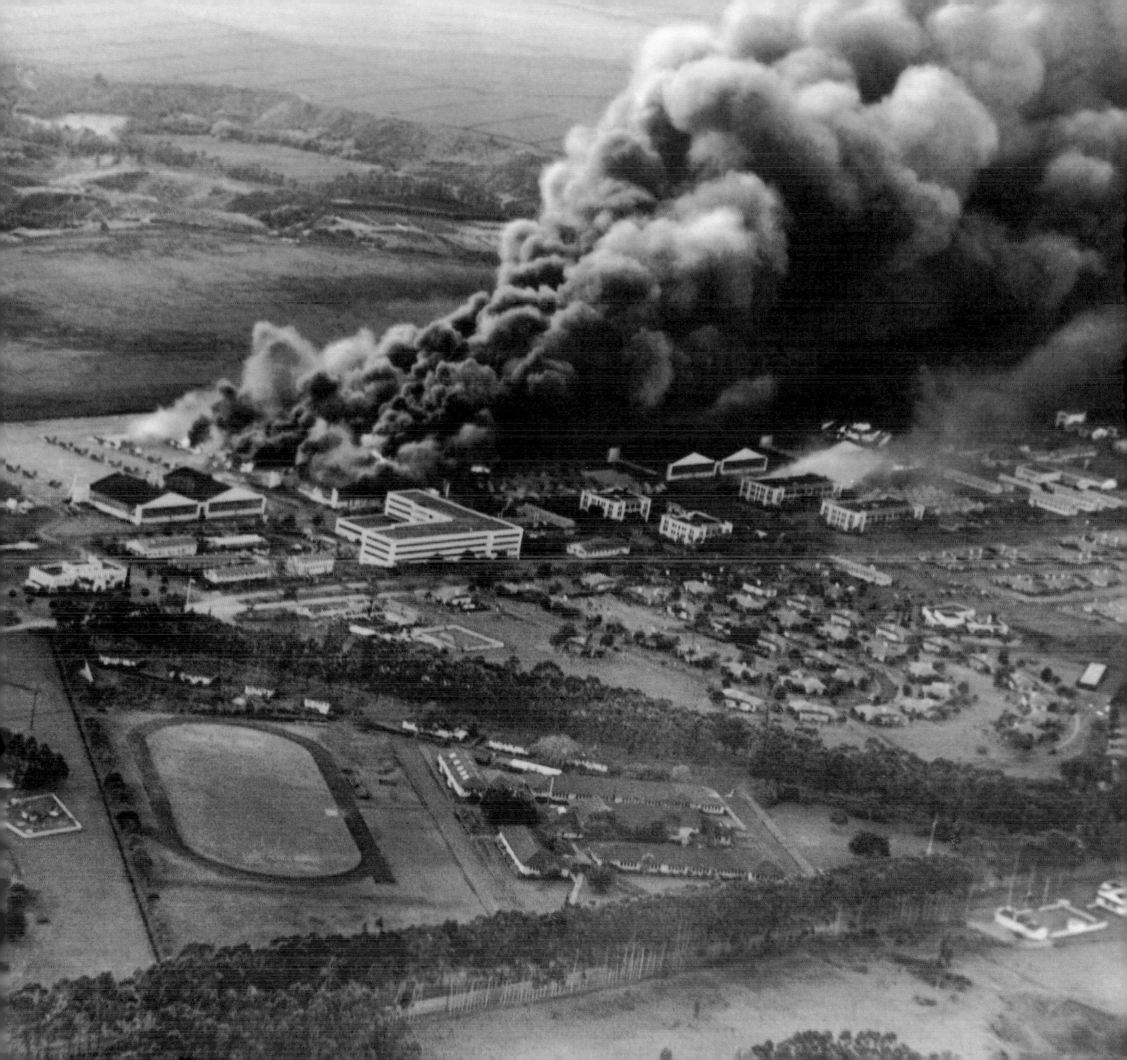

ABOVE: **Carnage at Wheeler Field. From his home on the base, Colonel William J. Flood, the field's commander, heard a loud thud, followed by another. Running outside, he saw a bomb explode in the depot area, and first thought someone on maneuvers had dropped it accidentally. Once he recognized the planes as Japanese, he headed for the flight line.**

Among the enlisted, Corporal Franklin Hibel of the 14th Pursuit Wing had just reached for his aloha shirt when machine-gun bullets crashed into the barracks, shattering windows, walls, and footlockers and hitting a few men still in their bunks.

LEFT: The first bombs to hit struck Hangar One and Hangar Three, seen here. The earth-shattering explosions turned the hangars into smoking, burning wrecks, blowing out skylights, windows, and the hangar doors and causing heavy casualties among the maintenance crews. Officers and enlisted men worked together to battle the fires, tend the wounded, and salvage equipment and supplies from the burning buildings. Though wounded, Staff Sergeant Charles A. Fay managed to move one plane out of a burning hangar. The smoldering remains of the tent area along Hangar Row can be seen on the left side of this photo; a burnt-out fuel truck is center right.

ABOVE: The new barracks of the 6th Pursuit Squadron, seen here, was also struck by dive-bombers the morning of the attack, inflicting heavy damage and casualties. The sleepy barracks quickly became the scene of grisly pandemonium, as the powerful blasts blew men out of the upper stories. Some men scrambled to the supply room for weapons and ammunition, some walked around dazed, and others helped the wounded and dying. To add to the misery, the building was not long after strafed by low-flying Japanese planes, killing one private, Donald D. Plant, as he moved wounded to the dispensary.

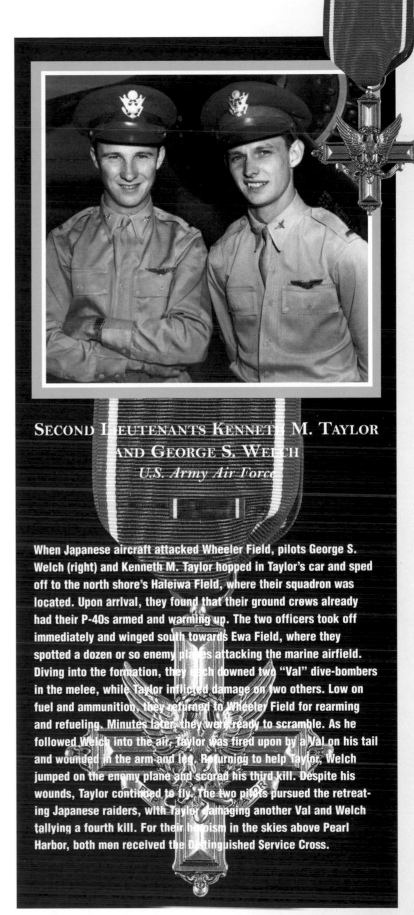

ABOVE: After dropping their bombs, the Japanese dive-bombers machine-gunned the parked aircraft and structures with incendiary bullets. Wheeler's P-40 Curtiss Warhawks and P-36 fighter planes were blown to bits, their burning parts scattered along the runway. This Warhawk was riddled by strafing fire from the dive-bombers.

LEFT: Many of the burning planes could not be saved. Once the enemy left, the immediate task was to salvage any aircraft that could be repaired. Sifting through the wrecked aircraft, resourceful mechanics remove spare parts to reuse in other, less damaged planes.

SECOND LIEUTENANTS KENNETH M. TAYLOR AND GEORGE S. WELCH
U.S. Army Air Force

When Japanese aircraft attacked Wheeler Field, pilots George S. Welch (right) and Kenneth M. Taylor hopped in Taylor's car and sped off to the north shore's Haleiwa Field, where their squadron was located. Upon arrival, they found that their ground crews already had their P-40s armed and warming up. The two officers took off immediately and winged south towards Ewa Field, where they spotted a dozen or so enemy planes attacking the marine airfield. Diving into the formation, they each downed two "Val" dive-bombers in the melee, while Taylor inflicted damage on two others. Low on fuel and ammunition, they returned to Wheeler Field for rearming and refueling. Minutes later, they were ready to scramble. As he followed Welch into the air, Taylor was fired upon by a Val on his tail and wounded in the arm and leg. Returning to help Taylor, Welch jumped on the enemy plane and scored his third kill. Despite his wounds, Taylor continued to fly. The two pilots pursued the retreating Japanese raiders, with Taylor damaging another Val and Welch tallying a fourth kill. For their heroism in the skies above Pearl Harbor, both men received the Distinguished Service Cross.

LEFT: **Private First Class Frank Rom had just stepped outside the huge mess hall at the center of the Consolidated Barracks for a smoke when the bombing started. He yelled a frantic warning to the soldiers still eating inside. The men headed for the exits, scattering tables, chairs, and trays of food in all directions, but it was too late. A bomb crashed through the roof and exploded, killing thirty-five men instantly. The survivors crawled to safety through the rubble.**

RIGHT: **Hickam Field's newest structure, the Consolidated Barracks, was a huge complex with ten wings serving as quarters for three thousand enlisted men. As Japanese dive-bombers swept in from three directions toward the barracks, Private First Class Robert P. Chase was awakened by the booming explosions, which Private Ira W. Southern mistook for artillery gunfire. A sudden explosion tore a huge hole in the barracks roof, sending shrapnel in all directions. Despite the sudden chaos, the men fought the fires, tended the wounded, and drew ammunition and guns from the armory.**

ABOVE: The damaged tail of Brigadier General Jacob H. Rudolph's personal B-18 bomber (known as "Bolo") stands in front of the burned and twisted framework of Hickam Field's Hangar Eleven. General Rudolph of the 18th Bomb Wing had scheduled extended training runs for a number of B-18 bombers that morning. When the Japanese dive-bombers came in, twenty-four men were at Hangar Eleven preparing the bombers for take-off. One of the first bombs scored a direct hit on the hangar, nearly wiping them all out. Twenty-two men died instantly and the other two were seriously injured.

ABOVE: **In Hickam Field's air control tower, Colonel William F. Farthing saw several aircraft approaching from the northwest. As they began their dive, Farthing remarked to a fellow officer: "Very realistic maneuvers by the Marine Corps." Then he saw the red "meatballs" on the wings and rushed out to sound the alarm. Seconds later, bullets and bombs tore into hangars, station buildings, and the neatly parked bombers, reducing much of the sprawling airbase into a smoking mass of confusion. Wrecked and burning aircraft littered the flight line, while strafing aircraft cut down men as they ran for cover. The oil storage area (seen here) behind the barracks was completely destroyed, as were the base chapel, the firehouse with its two engines, the new steam plant, and the enlisted men's beer hall, known as the Snake Pit.**

LEFT: In this view across the Parade Grounds at the officers' quarters, thick clouds of billowing black smoke from Battleship Row form a backdrop to the devastation at Hickam Field.

Lieutenant Colonel William C. Farnum had been awakened earlier by Sergeant John "Red" Davis, who shouted, "This is it! The Japs are here!" Taking Farnum's light gray Mercury, they sped towards the hangars, where they joined the officers and men struggling to move undamaged planes, fight fires, disperse gas trucks, and aid the wounded.

Back at the barracks, Sergeant Wilbur K. Hunt was trying to set up a couple of .50 caliber machine guns in a bomb crater. A bomb had freed the prisoners from the nearby guardhouse and they offered to help Hunt, who immediately put his new gun crew to work.

ABOVE: The first bombs to fall on Pearl Harbor were dropped from nine *Shokaku*-borne dive-bombers led by Lieutenant Commander Kauichi Takahashi. They hit Hangar Six (seen here), on the southeastern tip of Ford Island, burning the hangar to its steel framework. Many seaplanes, PBY-5 Catalinas and OS2U-3 Kingfishers, were turned into charred wrecks. Admiral William R. Furlong, out for his morning stroll on the flagship USS *Oglala*, saw the bombs dropped. Initially believing they were from American pilots on a practice run, he was jarred into reality by the explosions. As one plane turned and flew by, he could see the red Japanese insignia on its wings. He shouted to his crew, "Japanese! Man your stations!" Of course, the men had seen the explosions, too, and were already manning their guns and closing watertight doors.

ABOVE: **At the Ford Island seaplane ramp, sailors belt machine-gun ammunition. Though absorbed in their work, a few continue to glance skyward, ready to give the warning and run for cover at the first sign of low-flying enemy planes. Many had already experienced strafing fire.**

Aviation machinist Mate Third Class Ernest Cochran had just returned to the barracks from his duties at Hangar Six when he heard the first explosions. Ordered to report to his squadron, Cochran climbed aboard a truck with twelve other sailors heading for the hangars. Their truck came under fire from a Japanese plane, forcing the men to take cover in a nearby ditch. They made it the rest of the way on foot.

ABOVE: **At 0757, sixteen torpedo bombers attacked the ships on the northwest side of Ford Island (center). The first six launched their torpedoes, with two striking the USS *Utah*, one the cruiser USS *Raleigh*, and three grounding into the Ford Island shoreline. The rest of the planes saw no carriers or battleships and veered off to seek bigger game. On the eastern side of the island, torpedo hits on the *West Virginia* and *Oklahoma* send huge geysers of water into the air.**

RIGHT: **This aerial view of Ford Island, looking northeast, shows the *Utah*, at the lower left of the island, already listing from two torpedo hits. Across the island, on Battleship Row, water geysers mark where the *Oklahoma* and *West Virginia* have been struck by torpedoes. One of the attacking planes (center) can been seen over the *Neosho*, a tanker, and another over the Navy Yard (top right). Lieutenant Jinichi Goto, who launched his torpedo at the *Oklahoma* in the opening minutes of the attack, later recalled, "I saw that I was lower than the crow's nest of the great battleship. As we flew over, my observer [rear gunner] reported a huge waterspout spring up. 'Atarimashita! [It hit!],' he cried."**

RIGHT: **At 0755, the light cruiser *Raleigh* was one of the first ships in the harbor hit by the Japanese raiders. Captain R.B. Simons was in his cabin having a cup of coffee when he heard and felt a dull explosion. He looked out the porthole and saw a towering water column amidships. A torpedo had slammed into her port side, immediately flooding the forward engine room and two fire-rooms; within seconds, the ship began to list heavily to one side. As the *Raleigh*'s crew scrambled to their battle stations, few had time to dress. Ensign John Beardall worked the port anti-aircraft guns in his red pajamas. Although some were in uniform, most remained in skivvies, aloha shirts, T-shirts, and other forms of informal attire. Here, the fleet tug USS *Sunnadin*, which came to the aid of the *Raleigh* with pumps, electricity, food, and fresh water, has secured a pontoon storage barge alongside the cruiser to help keep her afloat.**

ABOVE: **The *Utah* strains at her mooring lines, only seconds before the lines snapped and she rolled over completely. At 0750, two torpedoes had slammed into her, blowing huge holes in her portside. Torrents of seawater rushed in and flooded her compartments and passageways. By 0805, the old ship had rolled over, taking fifty-seven men to a watery grave.**

RIGHT: **This Japanese aerial photo of the western side of Ford Island depicts, from left, the undamaged light cruiser USS *Detroit*; her sister ship, the badly damaged *Raleigh*; the capsized hull of the *Utah*; and the lightly damaged seaplane tender USS *Tangier*.**

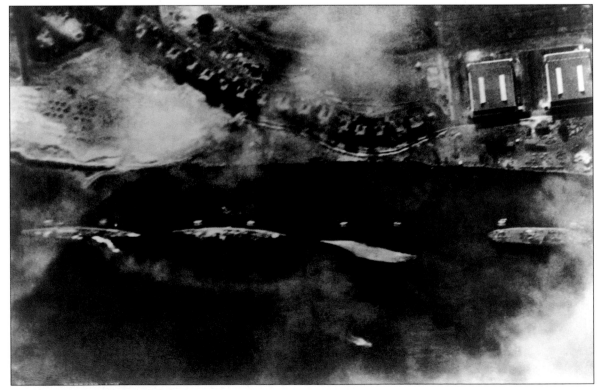

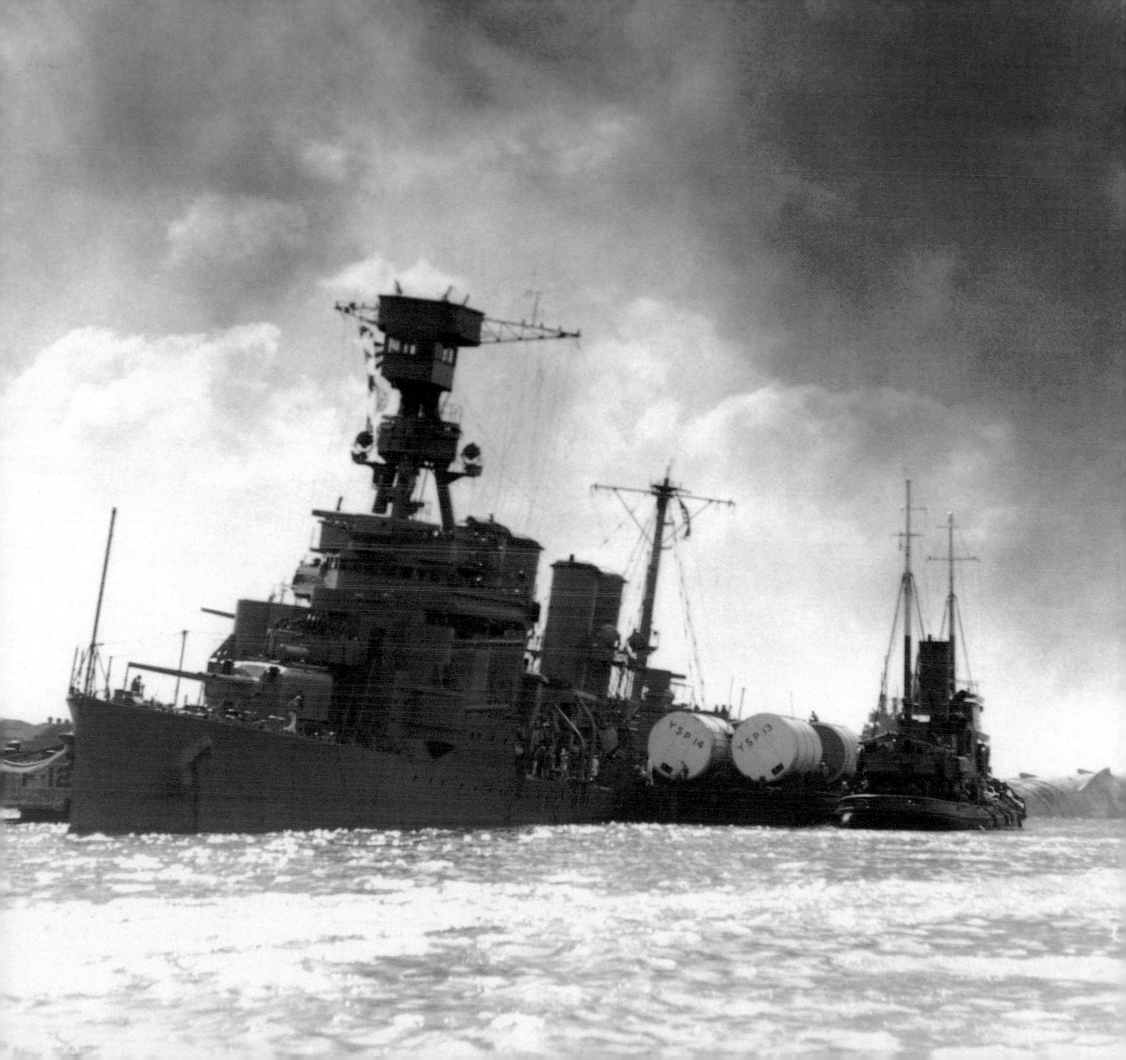

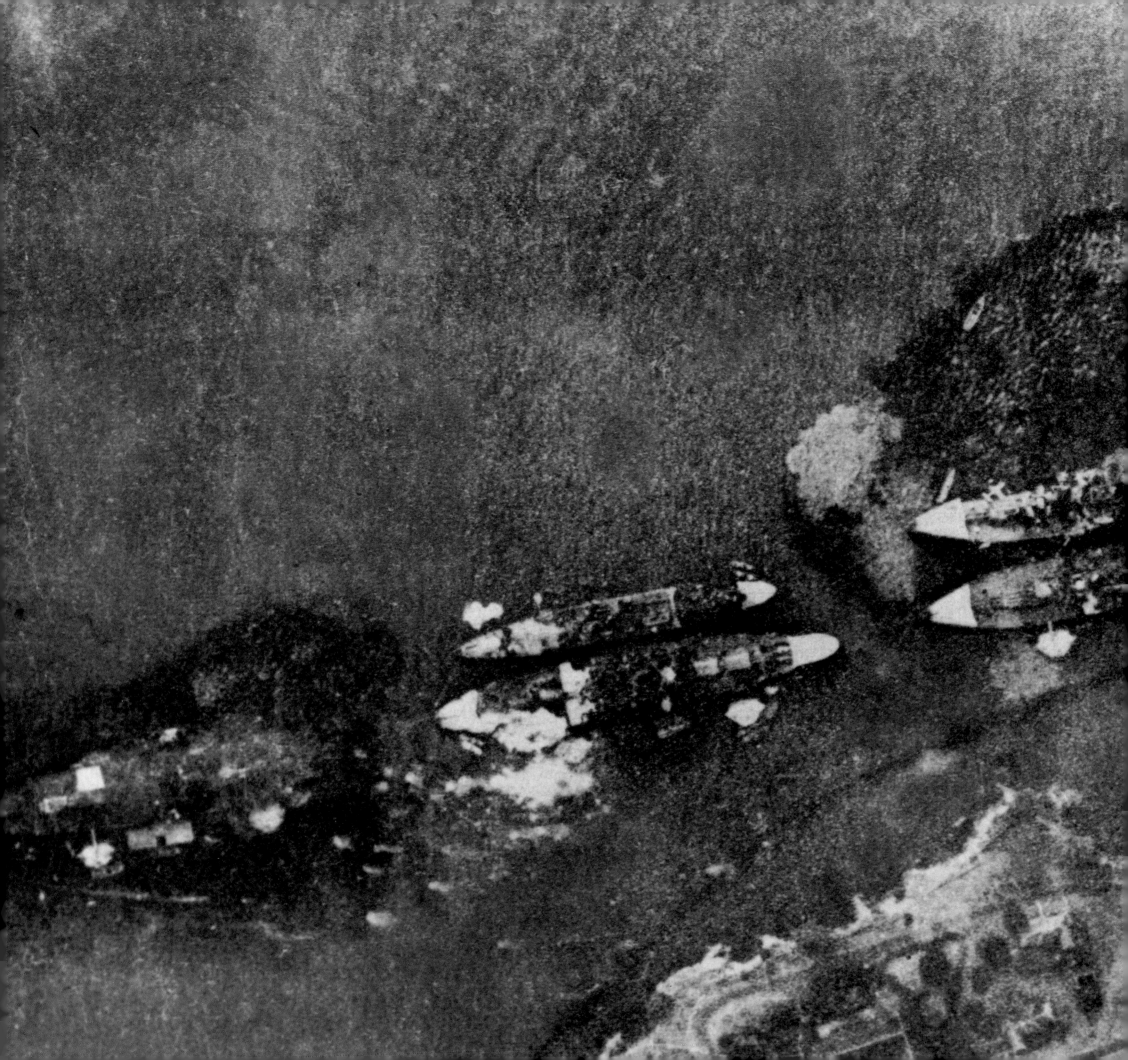

LEFT: **AT 0805,** a high-level bomber from the carrier *Kaga* ("Increased Joy") took this photo of Battleship Row. The *Oklahoma* (far right, top) and the *West Virginia* (second from right, top) are seen listing heavily and spilling large amounts of bunker fuel into the harbor. The *Arizona* (second from left, bottom) has been hit aft on the quarterdeck, near turret number four, and the *Vestal* (second from left, top) is hit forward of the bridge. Both the *Arizona* and the *Vestal* were hit by 1,756-pound (795.5kg) No. 80 armor-piercing bombs dropped from this flight of five B5N2 Nakajima bombers. Three near misses caused light damage. The *Nevada* (far left) has already been hit near the bow of the ship.

ABOVE LEFT: Seconds after a fatal bomb had penetrated four decks and detonated the *Arizona's* forward powder magazines, black smoke belched from the ship's single smokestack. The towering plume of smoke from the explosion, seen and heard for miles around the harbor, gave rise to the myth that a bomb went down the smokestack. In fact, the cover and armored grating from the stack were recovered intact, with no evidence of any bomb damage. It is most likely that the force of the explosion damaged the air intakes in the ship's fire rooms, causing a deadly backdraft.

ABOVE RIGHT: Seven seconds after the bomb's impact, the forward part of the *Arizona* erupted into a giant fireball, with the entire ship soon a blazing, doomed wreck. The powerful explosion and searing heat cut down hundreds of men in an instant and ignited the fuel oil spilling from the wounded ship into the water.

RIGHT: Survivors from the *Arizona*, mostly from the aft section of the vessel, made their way to the quarterdeck to abandon ship. Marine Private Russell J. McCurdy had just climbed the *Arizona's* mainmast to the fire-control compartment (top of the mast) when the ship was rocked by the violent explosion. McCurdy, Major Allan Shapely, Corporal Earl C. Nightingale, Seaman Don E. McDonald, and about ten others were all thrown to the compartment's deck. Still alive, they immediately abandoned the mainmast to escape the intense heat, with McCurdy badly burning his hands on the hot railing during the climb down. Making their way over to the quay, they had to step past many charred, dead bodies on the quarterdeck. They finally escaped into the oil-soaked water, less than 100 yards (30.5m) from shore. Although Nightingale couldn't swim—Shapely and McDonald had to tow him—they all made it safely to Ford Island.

FOLLOWING PAGES: **The dying *Arizona* settles on the harbor bottom, with her flag still flying proudly. When the bombs hit, the men had been preparing for church services, planning their shore leave, or undertaking duties aboard ship. Boatswain's Mate John Anderson, up early rigging awnings for the church service, was on the less-devastated quarterdeck and survived. Most were not as lucky. The blast killed 1,177 sailors and marines. Seaman First Class Michael Zwarun, Jr., held on drunk and disorderly charges for a general court-martial, was locked in the brig when the ship went down.**

CAPTAIN FRANKLIN VAN VALKENBURGH
United States Navy

Both Captain Franklin Van Valkenburgh, Commanding Officer, *USS Arizona*, and Rear Admiral Isaac C. Kidd, Battleship Division Commander, spent Saturday evening aboard the *Arizona*. Shortly before 0800 on December 7, Japanese planes roared overhead. The explosions of bombs and torpedoes shattered the peaceful Sunday morning. Racing to his duty station on the navigation bridge, Captain Van Valkenburgh immediately began to direct the ship's defense. When general quarters was sounded, Ensign Douglas Hein ran to the signal bridge, where Admiral Kidd stood at his station, before joining Captain Van Valkenburgh and a quartermaster in the pilothouse. The quartermaster urged the captain to take cover in the armored conning tower, but Van Valkenburgh refused. Suddenly, a violent explosion shook the ship. As flames shot through the shattered windows, men were thrown onto the deck. Dazed and shaken, Ensign Hein stumbled through the smoke and flames to escape. He was the sole survivor from the bridge area. After the fires were extinguished two days later, a search recovered only the class rings of Captain Van Valkenburgh and Admiral Kidd. They were both posthumously awarded the Medal of Honor for their gallantry and devotion to duty.

ABOVE: **A minute after the first attack by the *Kaga* bombers, another group of five high-level horizontal bombers from the *Hiryu* ("Flying Dragon"), led by Lieutenant Commander Tadashi Kusumi, attacked the damaged *Arizona* and *Vestal*. Flying at about 10,400 feet (3,161.6m), Kusumi's bombardier, Lieutenant Shojiro Kondo, released the fatal bomb that destroyed the *Arizona*. Kusumi's squadron also scored a direct hit on the *Vestal* (bottom), with three bombs causing lighter damage to both vessels. In this photo taken in a later bombing run, the *Oklahoma* has rolled over (upper center), while smoke from the mortally wounded *Arizona* obscures the rest of Battleship Row.** RIGHT: **The *Arizona's* bridge has collapsed at an eerie angle into the smoldering void left by the destructive explosion. There was only one survivor forward of the bridge. Nearly a thousand men were lost in the first few seconds, with another two hundred mortally wounded; only 337 survived.**

COMMANDER CASSIN YOUNG
United Stated Navy

Of Pearl Harbor's fifteen Congressional Medal of Honor recipients, Commander Young was one of only four who survived the attack. His citation, "for distinguished conduct in action, outstanding heroism and utter disregard of his own safety, above and beyond the call of duty," describes his courageous efforts to stay with the ship under his command, the USS *Vestal*. When the attackers first struck, the citation goes on, "Cmdr. Young proceeded to the bridge and later took command of the 3-inch anti-aircraft gun. When blown overboard by the blast of the forward magazine explosion of the *USS Arizona*, he swam back to his ship. The entire forward part of the *Arizona* was a blazing inferno, with oil afire on the water between the two ships. As a result of two bomb hits, the *Vestal* was afire in several places, was settling and taking on a list. Cmdr. Young, with extreme coolness and calmness, moved his ship to an anchorage distant from the *Arizona*, and subsequently beached the *Vestal* upon to save his ship."

Promoted to Captain on February 19, 1942, Young was assigned to command the heavy cruiser USS *San Francisco*. He was killed in action nine months later when his cruiser led the attack against a superior enemy force approaching the Solomon Islands' Guadalcanal. He was awarded the Navy Cross posthumously for this action.

ABOVE: **After the *Vestal* had been hit by aerial bombs, the executive officer gave the order to abandon ship. The skipper, Commander Young, who had been blown overboard, climbed back on board and shouted to the men, "Come on back! We're not giving up this ship yet!" Most returned and began hacking at the hawsers tying the repair ship to the blazing *Arizona*. "Turkey" Graham, an aviation mechanic, slashed the last line with a fire ax. The *Vestal* was moved into the shallows and beached to prevent her from sinking.**

RIGHT: **This photo, taken from an automobile speeding through Aiea past East Loch, shows the cloud of smoke rising from the dying *Arizona*.**

ABOVE: In the early moments, a flight of high-level bombers from the *Soryu*, led by Lieutenant Heijiro Abe, scored two hits on the *Tennessee*, seen here on the right, though only one bomb detonated. It exploded in the middle gun of turret two, killing four and rendering the turret inoperative. Shortly afterward, the *Arizona* blast threw burning debris and oil onto the *Tennessee*, starting fires on the stern and quarterdeck and igniting the fuel oil leaking into the harbor from the stricken ships. Fires breaking out inside the ship from the intense heat further warped and buckled the plating above the waterline, opened seams, and loosened rivets. When the *West Virginia* sank, she wedged the *Tennessee* hard against the mooring quays, so the ship could not move. To keep the burning oil away from the ship until all fires were out, the crew played water hoses over her stern and turned the ship's propellers over at 5 knots.

BELOW: As torpedoes began smashing into the *West Virginia*, men struggled to reach their battle stations. Heavy flooding gave the ship a list, making it difficult to walk without holding onto something. Given the order to counter-flood, Lieutenant Claude V. Ricketts, Boatswain's Mate Garnett Billingsley, and two others flooded the voids on the starboard side, thus correcting the dangerous list. The ship settled on the harbor bottom without capsizing, avoiding the fate of the *Oklahoma*.

On the bridge, Captain Mervyn S. Bennion was not as lucky. Mortally wounded by a piece of shrapnel, he was beyond all help and knew it. As the fires crept up to the bridge, all regular exits were cut off. Bennion ordered his men to leave him and save themselves, winning the Medal of Honor for his courage above and beyond the call of duty.

RIGHT: Although the crew had been fighting the *West Virginia's* raging fires for more than an hour, the ship was still a sea of flames and covered with choking black smoke. With all power gone, ammunition exploding from the heat, and burning oil drifting down from the *Arizona*, the time came to abandon ship. Here, her main deck is just barely above the surface of the water; the bridge and foremast are engulfed in flame and smoke. From the small boat (foreground), a marine, John J. Latko, leans over to pull a badly burned sailor, Fireman Third Class William Moore, out of the water. Marine Bugler Richard I. Fiske stands on the bridge (top), wearing a steel helmet. Some were trapped on the bridge until Ensign Henry Graham tossed up a line; they climbed down hand over hand safely to the *West Virginia's* deck. Latko, Moore, and Fiske would not see each other again for fifty years, until December 7, 1991, when they were reunited at Pearl Harbor.

MESS ATTENDANT SECOND CLASS
DORIS MILLER
United States Navy

Doris Miller, known as "Dorie" to his shipmates aboard the *West Virginia*, was collecting laundry when the alarm for general quarters was sounded. He raced to his battle station only to find it untenable due to torpedo damage. Miller was then ordered to the bridge to help move the ship's mortally wounded Commanding Officer, Captain Bennion. Unable to carry this out due to hazardous conditions, Miller and Lieutenant Junior Grade F.H. White manned the two machine guns forward of the conning tower, firing at an incoming flight of dive-bombers. As smoke and fire engulfed the bridge, the dying captain ordered the men to leave him and save themselves. When the attack was over, White and Miller teamed up again on the quarter-deck to haul men out of the oily waters, saving the lives of many. For his courage, Miller was awarded the Navy Cross.

As a crewmember of the escort carrier USS *Liscombe Bay*, Miller was killed in action on November 24, 1943, when that ship sank due to enemy action.

LEFT: **When the *Arizona* blew up, Chief Electrician's Mate Harold North, aboard the battleship *Maryland* (on the left), thought the end of the world had come. The *Maryland* was moored inboard from the *Oklahoma*, which bore the brunt of the torpedo hits. Just two 16-inch (40.6cm) armor-piercing aerial bombs smashed into the *Maryland*, causing minor damage, killing three men, and wounding thirteen. The first hit the forecastle and tore a hole twelve feet by twenty feet (3.6mX6.1m), damaging compartments below, and the second entered the hull below the waterline, causing considerable flooding. In the center of this photo, small ships fight fires on the sunken *West Virginia*. The capsized hull of the *Oklahoma* is to the right of the *Maryland*.**

ABOVE: **A curtain of oily black smoke from the *Arizona* obscures most of Battleship Row. The small boats darting around the harbor rescued men in the water and transported the wounded to the hospital ship *Solace* or to the Naval Hospital. Before the attack, Seaman First Class Leslie Vernon Short, a twenty-two-year-old from Garden City, Kansas, had gone up to a machine-gun station in the *Maryland's* foretop, looking for a quiet place to write letters home and address Christmas cards. He noticed some planes diving on the Naval Air Station nearby and thought that they were U.S. Navy planes in a mock dive. Once he realized they were Japanese, he loaded the .50 caliber machine gun and opened fire at two torpedo planes. It was before the call to battle stations had sounded, and the planes had just released their torpedoes at Battleship Row. Short saw smoke and flames burst from the first plane, which veered left and fell towards the hospital.**

LEFT: The overturned hull of the *Oklahoma*—hit by as many as nine torpedoes, one after the other in quick succession—can be seen lying next to the *Maryland* on Battleship Row. The torpedoes tore the *Oklahoma*'s port side open, she flooded rapidly, and with no time for the crew to counter-flood, she rolled over 158 degrees until her masts and superstructure hit the mud of the harbor bottom. Navy Chaplain Lieutenant Junior Grade Aloysius H. Schmitt was in his quarters vesting himself for Sunday mass. When the order to abandon ship was given, several men ran into the chaplain's room, which they knew had a porthole. The padre insisted that the men escape through the porthole ahead of him. As the last man climbed through, the porthole rolled beneath the surface and water rushed in, trapping Chaplain Schmitt. His gallant sacrifice saved the lives of fifteen sailors. Schmitt was awarded the Navy and Marine Corps Medal posthumously.

SEAMAN FIRST CLASS JAMES RICHARD WARD
AND ENSIGN FRANCIS C. FLAHERTY
United States Navy

When the air-raid siren sounded, the gun crews quickly manned their battle stations in the *Oklahoma*'s four main 14-inch (35.6cm) gun turrets. Although the ship's large guns had no role to play in repelling an air attack, the men remained at their posts, feeling the impact of each torpedo crashing into the ship. It wasn't long before the *Oklahoma* was severely damaged. Soon she listed dangerously, all power was lost, and the lights went out.

Ensign Flaherty (right) ultimately had no choice but to give the order for his men to abandon ship, but because of the hits that had opened up her port side, the battleship had begun to capsize rapidly. As the ship rolled under the surface, the crew was trapped inside the turret. Several men managed to pry open a hatch while the ship was turning over, and the air pressure inside prevented the water from completely filling the darkened interior of the turret as it went under.

The twenty-two-year-old Flaherty called for a volunteer to assist him in helping the others to escape. Seaman Ward, two years younger, responded first. The two men held their flashlights in the dark turret as it filled with water, fixing the direction of the open hatch so the men could swim out and to the surface. Neither Flaherty nor Ward escaped, and both were awarded the Congressional Medal of Honor for their "conspicuous devotion to duty and extraordinary courage and complete disregard of [their] own [lives], above and beyond the call of duty."

Ensign Herbert Charpiot Jones
United States Navy

★ ★ ★

On the morning of December 7, Ensign Jones was preparing to catch the liberty boat to Waikiki Beach for a day ashore with fellow sailors. When the call to general quarters blared over the speakers, he ran to his battle station at a 5-inch (12.7cm) ammunition handling room. As soon as he reached his post, Ensign Jones formed an ammunition detail with two other ensigns, W.F. Cage and I.W. Jefferies, and the enlisted personnel already manning the station. As they worked the ammunition hoists below deck near a 5-inch magazine, a Japanese 16-inch (40.6cm), 1,756-pound (795.5kg) bomb crashed through the upper decks and exploded in their vicinity. Ensign Jefferies was among the nearly fifty men killed instantly by the blast, while Ensign Jones was mortally wounded.

Despite their own injuries, Jones's shipmates tried to remove him from the area. "Leave me alone," he protested. "I'm done for. Get out of here before the magazines go off." The men escaped the inferno, but could not save Ensign Jones. He was awarded the Medal of Honor posthumously for his gallantry.

ABOVE: The fleet oiler *Neosho* (right) was moored at the gasoline wharf on Ford Island, next to the *California* (center). The crew had worked through the night to unload a cargo of high-octane aviation gas when the first wave of Japanese aircraft arrived. Commander John S. Philips knew if his ship was hit, with the remainder of its highly volatile cargo still on board, it would turn the already blazing inferno of Battleship Row into a holocaust. He ordered the lines cast off ashore, but no dock crew was on hand. "Chop those lines!" Philips ordered the crew on board. At 0842, the ship slowly backed into the channel, past the smoldering *California* and barely clearing the overturned hull of the *Oklahoma*. It found a safer berth at Merry Point. The huge column of smoke hides the rain of destruction on Battleship Row.

OPPOSITE: At 0840, a towering column of black ugly smoke rises over Battleship Row from the blazing infernos onboard the wounded *Arizona* and *West Virginia*. When the servicemen on leave received news of the attack, they struggled to return to their posts or ships however they could—in some cases ingeniously and in some heroically. Due to the chaotic circumstances, they had to use any method of transportation they could find: cars, taxis, motorcycles, bicycles, and any kind of truck. Some walked and a few even swam. Sailors who made it to the fleet landings hitched rides in small boats like the one seen here, which is ferrying a group of men to their ships.

Seen from the signal tower on Ford Island, a towering pillar of black oily smoke rises skywards from the stricken battleships *Arizona* and *West Virginia*. Smoke also spews from the heavily damaged *California*, at the right of the photograph, which had taken a bomb hit around 0825. As flames raged through the second deck, Pharmacist's Mate William Lynch smashed open lockers in the ship's sickbay, vainly searching for morphine to give to the seriously wounded. To keep the guns firing, Chief Radioman Thomas Reeves ran through a burning passageway to a 5-inch (12.7cm)-ammunition handling room. Passing the shells by hand, the twenty-year veteran was soon overcome by the smoke and died at his station. For his bravery and devotion to duty, he was awarded the Congressional Medal of Honor.

ABOVE: **The men on the bridge of the *California* (seen here from Ford Island) saw the first explosions on the seaplane base and immediately sounded the general alarm, sending the crew scurrying to their posts. Several machine guns opened fire at torpedo bombers coming in from Merry Point. Yeoman Durrell Conner saw the first torpedo hit aft on the port beam and was sent reeling. The next one exploded seconds later, slamming into the hull forward of the bridge. Water and oil surged through the ship, flooding lower decks and knocking the power plant and forward air compressor stations out of action. The ship quickly began to list to port. The ship's medical officer, Commander J.D. Jewell, badly burned on the face and arms, would not leave his post and continued to treat the burned and wounded casualties. He survived, and was awarded the Navy Cross for his bravery.**

FOLLOWING PAGES: **Dive-bombers from the carrier *Soryu* targeted the *California*. One bomb crashed through the deck on the starboard side into the second deck, exploding in an anti-aircraft ammunition magazine and killing fifty-three men. Damage-control parties had restored power and brought some fires under control when they faced another threat to the ship's safety: burning oil and heavy acrid smoke from the wounded ships on Battleship Row had drifted down and engulfed the *California*. As more fires started on board, Captain J.D. Bunkley thought the ship was endangered and gave the order to abandon ship. The crew began making for the shore. Barely ten minutes later, though, the wind blew the flames clear. The skipper urged the crew back to fight the fires and save the ship. The crew was a little slow getting back to the damaged vessel when two sailors on board, noting that the flag had not been raised, hoisted the colors. A big cheer went up and the crew began streaming back.**

LEFT: As they approached the island on the morning of the attack, a flight of B-17 bombers arriving from the mainland saw a group of planes coming towards them. Major Truman H. Landon assumed that the U.S. Army had come out to greet them—until the planes suddenly opened fire on them. Realizing they were Japanese, the B-17s, with no ammunition aboard (in order to stow more fuel for the long flight), scattered. Sergeant Lee Embree took this photo of two Aichi dive-bombers after they had made a strafing pass at his plane.

BELOW: Two Japanese planes circle the crash site of an SBD Dauntless scout plane, marked by a column of smoke. At 0645 that morning, the carrier USS *Enterprise* had launched a flight of eighteen SBDs to patrol ahead of the ship and then fly on to Ford Island, where some of the men planned to join their families. Flying into the onslaught, they were mauled by the Japanese fighters. Only twelve made it safely to land.

LEFT: In the distance, a lone B-17 Flying Fortress passes over Aiea Heights looking for a safe place to land. The group of twelve B-17s had been expected to arrive on the morning of December 7; when the radar operators spotted the Japanese Air Armada, the attacking planes were mistaken for the American bombers. When the B-17s arrived, low on fuel, they had to land where they could: Lieutenant Frank Brostrom landed his on the Kahuku Golf Course; two bombers managed to land at the small army airfield at Haleiwa; and Lieutenant Robert Richards crash-landed his at Bellows Field.

The previous night, the Honolulu radio station KGBM had stayed on the air late playing Hawaiian music as a homing signal for the bombers coming in from the West Coast of the United States; unfortunately, the Japanese Air Armada had enjoyed the same directional beacon.

ABOVE: General Short's sabotage alert was in full force, with the bombers at Hickam Field lined up in neat rows alongside the main runway. That morning the hangars stood silent, but the control tower, near the left end of the hangar line, hummed with excitement; several officers wanted to see the arrival of the B-17s from the mainland. To have twelve of them come in at once was a big event indeed. Then all hell broke loose. The eight bombers that actually managed to land at Hickam had to time their approach between bombing and strafing runs.

ABOVE: Captain Raymond E. Swenson was circling and attempting to land at Hickam Field when his B-17 was strafed, probably by Lieutenant Masanobu Ibuski, a Zero pilot from the *Akagi*. One bullet set off the magnesium flares in the bomber's radio compartment, starting a fire in the midsection of the aircraft. The burning plane landed heavily on the tarmac, causing the tail section to break off as it skidded to a stop. The crew ran for shelter amid a hail of bullets. The only casualty was Lieutenant William R. Shick, mortally hit by a strafing Zero as he ran down the runway.

LEFT: **Seen from across the channel, clouds of smoke from the conflagration on the destroyer *Shaw* in the floating dry dock darken the skies. To the left, smoke also pours from the damaged cruiser *Helena* and the blazing destroyers USS *Cassin* and USS *Downes*. The capsized minelayer *Oglala* (foreground) lies next to Ten-Ten Dock. That morning, the *Oglala* had been tied up alongside the *Helena* when Seaman Robert Hudson saw a torpedo plane come in at fifty feet (15.2m) above the water and release its deadly missile towards his ship. The torpedo went under the *Oglala* and slammed into the *Helena's* engine room, killing nearly twenty men instantly. The blast caved in the thin sides of the *Oglala's* thirty-five-year-old hull and both ships began taking on water.**

RIGHT: **As the flooding spread rapidly through the *Oglala* (on its side), Admiral Furlong hailed two tugs nearby for assistance. They came alongside and secured her to the dock, but with the ship listing nearly 20 degrees, the men had to fight to maintain their footing. The lines holding the ship to the dock began to snap, and Furlong ordered "Abandon ship!" As the ship heeled over, the men walked across her sides onto the pier. Amazingly, no lives were lost aboard the *Oglala*.**

Above: **Looking down Ten-Ten Dock, the capsized *Oglala* (center) and cruiser *Helena* (behind it) lie next to the dock. The smoke drifting across the harbor comes from the burning destroyers *Cassin* and *Downes*, and from the battleship USS *Pennsylvania* (on blocks in the dry dock). Once the *Oglala's* crew were safely on the pier, the ship's doctors and medical personnel set up a first-aid station to help the wounded from other ships. Some of the minelayer's crew had salvaged a few machine guns and set them up on the pier; others were assigned to repair parties aboard the *Helena* and nearby ships.**

Above: This dramatic view of the devastation on Ford Island is seen from the corner of Puliki Place and Aiea Heights Drive, overlooking the harbor's northern rim. Witnessed by thousands of locals in the surrounding hills, the assault on Pearl Harbor created fear and confusion among inhabitants of the island. The bursts of anti-aircraft fire pictured here (above the clouds) probably offered small consolation to anxious islanders, even though it indicated that the ships' guns were finally fully manned.

Left: Soaring through the skies of Pearl Harbor, a wounded Japanese A6M2 Zero fighter trails smoke after being struck during a strafing run over Hickam Field; the plane was last seen heading out to sea, where it probably crashed.

In 1941, the Zero was the Japanese Navy's newest fighter and could outmaneuver any plane based on Oahu. During the raid, the Zeros were deployed to protect the Japanese bombers from the American pursuit planes that rose to meet them in battle.

BELOW: After the attack began, the *Curtiss'* gun crews were firing at the raiders within five minutes. At 0836, a periscope was sighted about seven hundred yards (638.4m) off the starboard quarter. *Curtiss* opened fire with her 5-inch (12.7cm) guns, hitting the sub's conning tower. The destroyer *Monaghan*, already underway, also spotted the intruder and tried to ram it. The ship grazed the sub, and as it surged by, Chief Torpedoman's Mate G.S. Hardon set his depth charges at thirty feet (9.1m) and let them go. The midget sub was destroyed in a terrific blast that knocked down nearly everybody on the deck of the *Monaghan*. Fireman Ed Creighton thought the ship had blown off its own fantail.

A few minutes later, a Japanese "Val" was diving towards the *Curtiss* when it was hit by the ship's guns and burst into flames. The crippled plane crashed, deliberately according to some witnesses, into the ship's crane, spraying the decks with burning gasoline and starting several fires.

ABOVE: The *Curtiss*, a large seaplane tender, was lying off Pearl City on the other side of Ford Island when it came under attack by a group of dive-bombers (circled). One bomb hit the mooring buoy astern, one fell short, and another overshot the *Curtiss*. Fragments from the near misses caused minor damage. The ship did not escape a fourth bomb, which hit the ship on the starboard boat deck, ripping through to the main deck near the hangar before it exploded. The blast caused considerable damage through six decks and ignited raging fires.

Ensign R.G. Kelly, who was in the immediate vicinity of (and wounded by) the explosion, led the amidships repair party until the fires were under control and then directed the removal of casualties. Twenty men lost their lives and another fifty were wounded; the ship, though damaged, did not sink.

LEFT: The smoking *Nevada* glides past Ten-Ten Dock during her epic attempt to escape the harbor. At 0755, Musician Oden McMillan and his twenty-three-man band had been on the ship's quarterdeck for the raising of morning colors when some of the band members noticed planes diving at the other end of Ford Island. As the Marine Guard hoisted the colors, the band began playing the "Star-Spangled Banner." At that exact moment, one of the torpedo planes that had launched at the *Oklahoma* angled upwards over the stern of the *Nevada* and the rear gunner opened fire, his machine gun spraying the decks. He did not hit anyone, but the flag was shredded on the flagstaff. The band kept on playing until the last note; only then did they leave for their battle stations.

BELOW: Lieutenant Lawrence E. Ruff was aboard the *Solace* waiting for morning mass when explosions were heard. The presiding priest immediately dismissed his flock, and Ruff caught a launch to his ship, the *Nevada*, which had already been seriously damaged. Preparations were made to get the wounded ship underway. The *Nevada* swung into action commanded by the senior officer present, Lieutenant Commander Francis J. Thomas, with Ruff as navigator and Chief Quartermaster Robert Sedberry the helmsman at the wheel. The ship slowly cleared the stern of the burning *Arizona* by forty feet (12.2m). The heat was so intense that the *Nevada*'s gunners shielded their shells with their bodies for fear that they might otherwise explode.

MACHINIST DONALD KIRBY ROSS
United States Navy

Machinist Donald Ross' battle station was in the forward dynamo room of the battleship *Nevada*. Early in the attack, the ship was damaged from a torpedo hit in the forward part of the ship. Ross forced his men to leave when the smoke, steam, and heat made their stations untenable. He manned the dynamo until he fell unconscious. He was rescued and brought around, but went back to secure the station. At 0840, the ship got under way. Ross went to the after dynamo station, where he eventually collapsed again. Once again he was carried out and resuscitated, and once again he returned to the dynamo room. Finally, he was ordered to abandon the post when the ship was intentionally run aground. He was awarded the Medal of Honor for distinguished conduct, extraordinary courage, and disregard for his own life during the attack on Pearl Harbor.

Ross retired as a Lieutenant Commander after 27 years' service in the navy.

LEFT: One of 23 Aichi "Val" dive-bombers led by Lieutenant Shigeo Makino from the *Kaga*, which had spotted the *Nevada* attempting to sail out of the harbor. If the Japanese could sink the battleship in the channel, the harbor would be blocked up for months. "The Japanese bombers swarmed down on us like bees," said Lieutenant Ruff. Several bombs struck the forecastle and exploded below decks, while another hit near the galley.

ABOVE: Finally, Lieutenant Commander Thomas received orders to abort the *Nevada*'s sortie to avoid being sunk in the channel. He decided to beach the ship near Hospital Point. Here, the *Nevada*, seriously damaged and with fires out of control, has just backed her engines and dropped anchor after easing her bow into the muddy shallows.

ABOVE: Aboard the seaplane tender *USS Avocet* (foreground), docked at the Naval Air Station, the gun crews man their battle stations. The men worked the guns deliberately and with apparent disregard for their own safety, firing 144 3-inch (7.6cm) AA (anti-aircraft) rounds at the attackers. Many of the ships in the harbor were concentrating anti-aircraft fire at the Japanese planes swooping down on the beleaguered *Nevada* (background).

A bomb hit had wiped out the crew of a 5-inch (12.7cm) anti-aircraft gun on the *Nevada*, killing or wounding most of the men in the adjoining gun battery as well. Gunner's Mate Robert E. Linnartz, though wounded himself, kept the gun in the adjoining battery in action, acting as sight-setter, pointer, and rammer until additional men were ordered up from belowdecks to help. The starboard AA ammunition conveyor was out of commission, so the men had to pass the shells from below by hand.

ABOVE: Though the *Nevada's* gallant attempt to reach the open sea ended in a grounding, she was the only battleship to get underway during the attack. Here, the wind and strong outbound harbor currents have caught the ship's stern and swung her completely around. Her bridge and superstructure are shrouded in the smoke and flames from her own guns and the raging fires caused by the bombings. At times, she almost disappeared from view when the explosions from near misses threw huge columns of water in the air. Dense layers of smoke from the burning destroyers in the dry dock and from the blazing *Shaw* nearby darken the skies overhead.

LEFT TOP: **As the heavily damaged *Nevada* ran aground near the floating dry dock, the *Shaw* was having her own problems in the dock. Her sailors fought the fires as best they could, but could not keep them from spreading. An unknown photographer on Ford Island captured one of the most memorable images of World War II, when the raging fires touched off the forward magazines of the *Shaw* at 0930. This spectacular explosion sent a huge fireball into the sky, with streamers of burning debris flying in all directions.**

Nearly a half mile (.8km) away, Seaman Ed Waszkiewicz watched from Ford Island; he thought he was safe until he looked up and saw one of the *Shaw's* 5-inch (12.7cm) shells tumbling end over end, arching toward him. He dove behind a fire truck just as the shell hit the concrete ramp near him. Luckily, it did not explode, merely bouncing a few hundred feet down the ramp into one of the hangars.

LEFT BOTTOM: **Compare the original photo of the destruction of the *Shaw* (top) with this retouched version. The bottom photo has been cropped to reduce the smoke, and the damaged battleship *Nevada* and small boat have been removed, as have the railing of the dredge line.**

Much of the early information released regarding damage and losses was subject to heavy censorship by the War Department, with the aim of keeping public morale high and making it difficult for the enemy to ascertain how much damage had been inflicted. After December 7, the media rarely showed pictures of American dead to the public. Not until November 1943, when the U.S. Marines suffered heavy casualties taking the island of Tarawa, was the public allowed to see multiple American fatalities.

CHIEF BOATSWAIN EDWIN JOSEPH HILL
United States Navy

During the height of the Japanese attack on Battleship Row, the senior officer aboard the *Nevada* gave the order to stand out to sea and cast off all lines. Chief Hill, a warrant officer and twenty-nine-year navy veteran, made it over to the quay and cast off the lines, with bullets peppering the ground around him. As the tide drew the battlewagon away from the quay, Hill dove into the water and swam back to his ship, clambering aboard.

Once Japanese dive-bombers concentrated their attack on the *Nevada*, the badly damaged ship received orders to run aground so she wouldn't block the channel if sunk. As Chief Hill was assisting in the anchor detail, a bomb exploded on the forecastle, killing an unknown number of men and blowing Chief Hill overboard to his death. For extraordinary courage and disregard for his own life, he received the Medal of Honor.

ABOVE: **The heavily wounded *Nevada* was pushed across the channel by the small vessels alongside, which are seen pouring streams of water onto the smoldering forward section of the battleship as they try to bring her fires under control. At the height of the Japanese onslaught the *Nevada* got underway in an effort to reach the open sea. As she sailed past the devastation and destruction on Battleship Row, the crews of other ships cheered at the sight of the big ship as she moved down the channel. After December 7, the *Nevada* would be known by a new nickname: "The Cheer-up Ship".**

OPPOSITE: **High above Pearl Harbor, the last of the raiders headed west to a rendezvous area near Kaena Point, from which location would begin the journey back to their carriers. This photo depicts the immediate aftermath of their visit. The *Nevada*, with the aid of several tugs, was moved across the channel to the hard sandy bottom of Waipio Peninsula. The yard tug *Hoga* is alongside fighting the smoldering fires on *Nevada*'s bow. With the danger of air attack apparently over, the men were released from battle stations to assist in fire fighting and begin the salvage work to save the ship. Men who had been belowdecks throughout the battleship's ordeal came on deck for some fresh air. One of them, Musician C.S. Griffin, recalled glancing at his watch. The time was 1000.**

ABOVE: **On Sunday morning, the destroyer *Shaw* (emitting the plume of smoke) was high and dry in the Navy Yard's floating dry dock for alterations to her depth-charge gear. As is customary for vessels undergoing an overhaul, most of the crew was ashore. At 0757, upon seeing the explosions on Ford Island, the men on board went to general quarters and commenced firing the machine guns at the enemy. The 5-inch (12.7cm) guns were not fired for fear that the concussion would knock the ship off the blocks of the drydock. At a height of 1,000 feet (304m), three dive-bombers from the *Akagi* released their deadly missiles almost simultaneously, all three smashing into the *Shaw* and starting fires.**

Above: **A D3A1 Aichi dive-bomber pulls up over the harbor after dropping its bomb on the ships in Ten-Ten Dock.**

Right: **Two huge columns of smoke drift southwards across the harbor. One spews from the raging fires on the destroyer *Shaw* (on the right) that followed the explosions in her magazines; the other is from her sister destroyers *Cassin* and *Downes* (left, just out of view). Berthed in the dry dock for repairs, both of the latter ships had been hit repeatedly by enemy dive-bombers. At the dry dock, civilian workers from the Navy Yard shops removed wounded sailors from the destroyers and brought in fire extinguishers, fire hoses, pickaxes, and other equipment to help fight the conflagrations.**

Following Pages: **The first two bombs struck the *Shaw* forward, crashing down through compartments and exploding in the crew's mess area. The third struck the port side of the bridge, passing through several decks and out the starboard side before exploding on the bottom of the dock. The *Shaw's* ruptured fuel tanks then ignited, sending huge pillars of thick smoke over the harbor. Attempts to fight the fires were hindered by damaged water mains, so a tender equipped with two fire monitors (hoses) came over from the Pan American Clipper terminal on Pearl City to pump water on the conflagration. The dry-dock officer and crew struggled valiantly to flood the dock; the port side valves were opened, but fire prevented the men from opening the starboard side, causing the dry dock to sink on an uneven keel.**

LEFT: **After fires from the magazine explosion aboard the *Shaw* were extinguished that afternoon, torn and twisted wreckage was all that remained of the vessel's bridge superstructure. Destruction of the two forward 5-inch (12.7cm) guns—as well as all ordnance, machinery, and equipment forward of the fire room bulkhead—was so complete, all that could be salvaged was an anchor windlass, one anchor, two chains, plus some chocks and bits. To have her forward bulkheads reinforced, the ship was moved to the marine railway at the Navy Yard. Work then began on salvaging the floating dry dock and small yard tug. Twenty-four men lost their lives and twenty-four were wounded in the Shaw's ordeal.**

OPPOSITE: **Murky clouds of black smoke shield the devastation on Battleship Row as the smoldering destroyer *Shaw* sits in the sunken, floating dry dock. The bow of the *Shaw* was almost severed from the hull by the tremendous blast, finally breaking away and toppling over when the dock sank. The dock's fuel tanks, filled the previous day, were ruptured from the explosions that destroyed the *Shaw*. The leaking fuel ignited, covering the waters around the ship with flaming oil. It was only due to a strong wind and the strenuous efforts of the remaining personnel that the after portion of the ship was saved. The small yard tug *Sotoyomo* was in the dock ahead of the *Shaw* and caught fire and sank when the larger ship's magazines blew up. Later, when the dry dock was raised, it was found that the dock's watertight integrity had been impaired by 155 holes in her structure.**

"AIR RAID PEARL HARBOR. THIS IS NOT A DRILL!"

LEFT: Sailors salvaging damaged seaplanes at the hangar area on Ford Island pause in their work to watch the huge fireball of smoke and flames from the horrific explosion aboard the *Shaw*.

Earlier that morning, thirteen-year-old Jerry Morton and his kid brother Don had sat on the enlisted men's landing at Pearl City, where they could see ships in every direction. Almost every morning that they were not in school, they went there to fish. The ships, planes, and sailors provided surroundings that never grew dull, and across from them lay Ford Island, where their stepfather, Aviation Ordnanceman First Class Theodore W. Croft, worked in the seaplane hangars. Croft was on duty that Sunday morning, and the boys anxiously waited through a tense week before discovering he had been killed by one of the first bombs to fall. Tragically, Croft was the only fatality at the seaplane base.

ABOVE: A B5N2 Nakajima high-level bomber from the *Zuikaku* has just completed its bombing mission over Hickam Field (bottom). The plane, piloted by Seaman First Class Masato Hatanaka, heads south to rendezvous for the return flight to the carriers. Giant clouds of smoke billow upwards from the ravaged ships on Battleship Row (right center) and from the Navy Yard fires that obscure Ford Island (directly beneath the bomber).

LEFT: **A Zero from the carrier *Kaga* swoops over the submarine base, heading toward Hickam Field (beyond the water towers) on a strafing run.**

At his Honolulu home earlier that morning, Lieutenant Commander Charles W. Wilkins, skipper of the submarine USS *Narwhal* (left), had been in bed reading Life magazine when a friend's wife telephoned. When she excitedly told him about the bombings at Pearl Harbor, he initially attributed them to an army drill. "It's real," she insisted. "I heard it on the radio!" Jumping into his car, Wilkins sped towards Pearl Harbor, where he saw for himself what was clearly no drill.

ABOVE: **At the submarine base, the gun crews on the submarine *Narwhal* (left, moored at Pier One) scan the skies for enemy planes. Across the channel, a curtain of thick black smoke hangs over the Navy Yard, where gun crews aboard the cruisers *Honolulu*, *St. Louis*, *San Francisco*, and *New Orleans* also watch the skies.**

Aboard the *New Orleans* (to the left of the hammerhead crane), electric power was out, so the crew passed ammunition by hand. As Chaplain Lieutenant Howell Forgy walked along the line of men to encourage them, he noticed Seaman Second Class Sam Brayfield's legs begin to buckle from carrying the heavy shells. Chaplain Forgy patted him on the shoulder and said, "Praise the Lord and pass the ammunition." For the rest of the morning, the men shouted that phrase as they fed shells to the gun crews. The words would later inspire songwriter Frank Loesser, who used the phrase as the title for one of the war's best-remembered songs.

BELOW: During a lull in the attack, a squad takes a breather on the parade grounds of the U.S. Marine barracks. That morning, Marine Gunner Floyd McCorcle was having breakfast with members of his company when a sharp blast rocked the building. As they instinctively ran to get their weapons, they could hear the bombs screaming down on nearby Hickam Field. Ordered to the parade grounds with their Springfield rifles, they formed circles of nine men to fire at the incoming planes.

ABOVE: Undamaged by the attack, the cruiser *Phoenix* is seen here sailing past the smoldering *Arizona* en route to the open sea. When the general alarm was sounded on the *Phoenix*, Machinist LeRoy Markley was in the machine shop writing Christmas cards. "For crying out loud," he thought. "Why are they having a drill on Sunday?" Another crewmember, Gunner's Mate Joseph St. Pierre, learned of the attack while in the shower. Told that the Japanese were "bombing the hell out of us," St. Pierre hurriedly pulled on a pair of shorts and ran, dripping wet, for his gun station.

RIGHT: **When the first bombs exploded, Private Robert C. Dresser had just returned from breakfast and stood outside the marine barracks (foreground) with a few buddies. As the call to arms was sounded, he saw marines dashing out of the barracks in disbelief, many donning their pants and shirts on the run.**

Later, marine Private First Class Robert Schawb was returning from a courier run to the Navy Yard message center when an explosion hurled him from his motorcycle. Although bruised, he managed to right the motorcycle and race back to his unit.

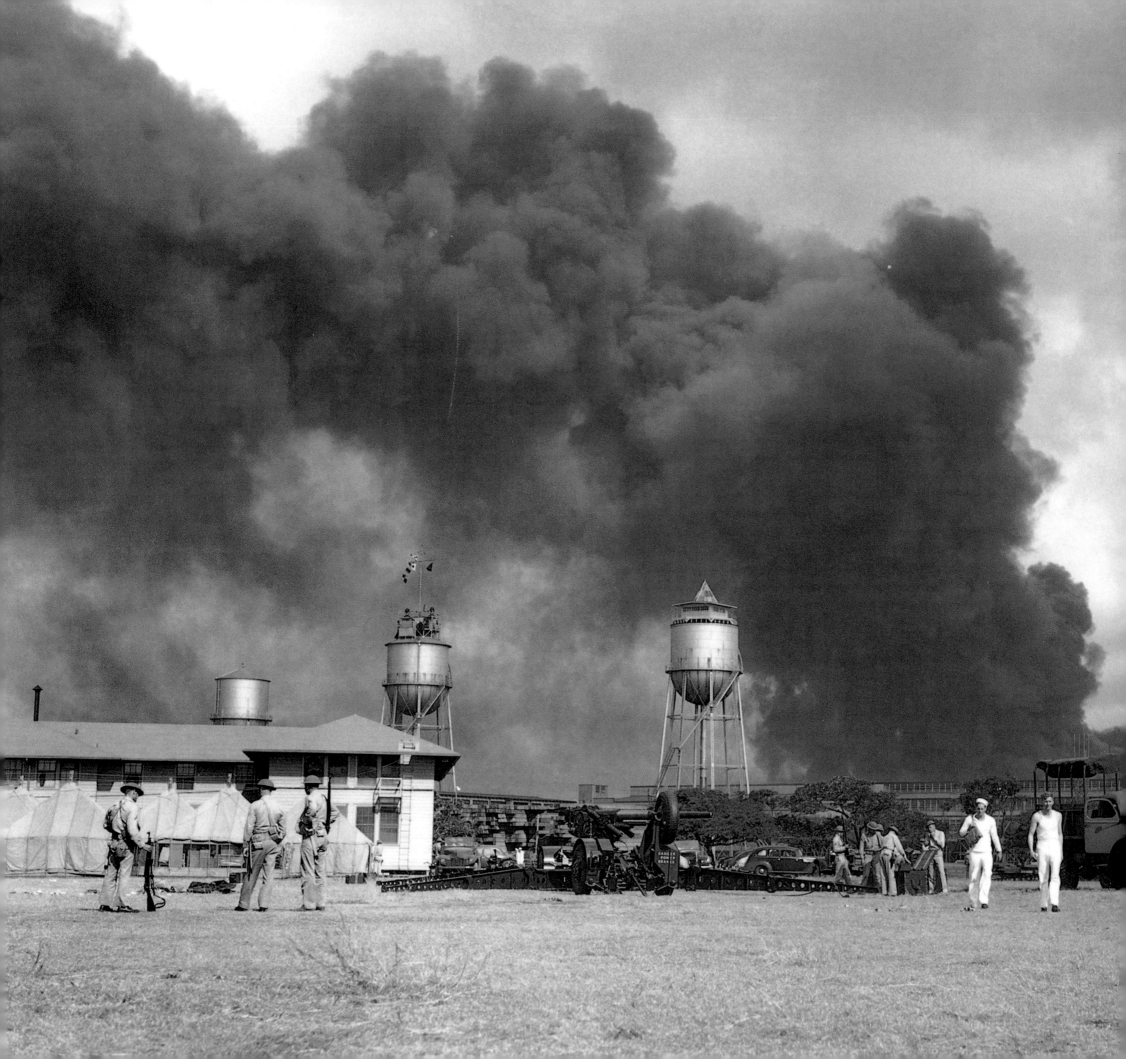

LEFT AND BELOW: **At the seaplane base on Ford Island, strafing Japanese aircraft sent the men on the ground running for whatever shelter was at hand. Storekeeper Jack Rogovsky and others dove under workbenches in the hangars, while Aviation Machinist's Mate Donald Crosby made a beeline for the safest place he could think of: the shower stalls. Outside, some of the flight crews jumped into a ditch alongside the runway that had been dug for a gas line. During a brief lull in the attack, Seaman James Layman joined a working party filling and loading sandbags onto a truck. The sandbags, wings and other aircraft parts, and machine guns salvaged from the damaged seaplanes were used to set up temporary anti-aircraft emplacements and bunkers for protection should the enemy planes return.**

LEFT: **Beyond the Navy Yard water towers, plumes of oily smoke rise from the burning *Arizona*. At the marine barracks (left, with tents), the servicemen's plans for the day changed abruptly with the wail of the air raid siren. As marines poured out of the barracks, Lieutenant James S. O'Halloran ordered a detail of men to haul, via tractor, the 3-inch (7.62mm) anti-aircraft guns to the parade grounds. Several marines can be seen here (center) attempting to bring one of those guns into action.**

CHAPTER THREE

ALL HANDS TURN TO

RIGHT: **Chief Boatswain's Mate L.M. Jahnsen was proud of his little ship, the** *YG-17* **(right), even though it was mounted with heavy duty water pumps instead of guns or armor. It had no name, only a symbol to designate it as a yard garbage scow (or "the honey barge," as it was affectionately called). When the first Japanese planes came in, Jahnsen was on his morning rounds, collecting refuse from various ships, and had just pulled up next to the** *Nevada.* **Receiving orders to help fight fires aboard the** *West Virginia* **(seen here), he maneuvered his lumbering craft alongside. Despite the danger from exploding ammunition, the** *YG-17* **and her crew gallantly sent streams of water into the inferno for eight hours, until ordered to assist at the** *Arizona.*

Like many Oahu servicemen that day, Lieutenant Kleiber S. Masterson was on leave ashore when he heard news of the air raid. After rushing back to Pearl Harbor, he discovered not only that the attack was over, but that his ship, the *Arizona*, was a blazing wreck. The last of the crew had already abandoned ship. For the rest of the day, Masterson mustered the *Arizona's* survivors to assist with the wounded.

Just before sunset, Masterson asked another *Arizona* survivor, Ensign Leon Grabowsky, to return to the ship with him. The ship's flag, Masterson felt, should be saved as a memento of the attack. As their motor launch eased alongside the *Arizona's* fantail, the battleship's forward section was still burning fiercely. Climbing aboard, they lowered the torn and oil-stained colors still flying from the ship's stern. They brought the flag over to the battleship *Maryland* and handed it to the officer of the deck, asking that it be saved. During the *Maryland's* own recovery efforts, though, the flag was lost, never to be seen again.

The U.S. Navy had been dealt a staggering blow, but not a crippling one. It could have been much worse: had the Japanese returned for a third strike against the untouched dry docks, Navy Yard installations, repair facilities, and oil-storage tanks, the salvage and repair of the damaged vessels would have been impossible. As it was, it took nearly three years to complete those efforts; only three of the nineteen damaged ships, the *Arizona, Utah*, and *Oklahoma*, never returned to service.

In the days immediately following the air raid, all hands—military and civilians alike—had to be pressed into service to begin the process of resurrecting what appeared to be a completely lost and shattered fleet.

ABOVE: On an overcast and rainy December 8, 1941, the cruiser *Northampton* enters Pearl Harbor after returning from a mission to Wake Island with the carrier *Enterprise*. As the *Northampton* moved to her berth, the crew stood silently on her decks, taking in the devastation that had been wrought by the Japanese raiders twenty-four hours earlier. Rear Admiral Raymond A. Spruance somberly observed the scene through the mist from the ship's bridge. Years of reading about and studying war had not prepared him for the sight. That evening, at his home on the naval base, he related his feelings to his wife, Margaret, and daughter, Meg, then never again spoke of that morning to anyone.

LEFT: **Seven men made it to their battle station in the port 5-inch (12.7cm) anti-aircraft gun director (right center) of the *Arizona*. When the ship blew up, one man simply vanished. Seaman First Class Don Stratton was badly burned, but survived, while Seaman First Class Russell Lott had wrapped himself in a blanket to keep from being scorched. As the surviving five shipmates staggered through the smoke, Lott used the blanket to help shield them all. A sailor on the *Vestal*, tied up alongside, tossed over a line and one by one, hand over hand, they made it across to the repair ship. Meanwhile, everyone forward of this director perished in a single searing flash, the front two-thirds of the ship a total loss.**

BELOW: The attackers inflicted heavy damage to the main hangars at Hickam Field as well as to the engine and equipment building and the main shop building—very little escaped unscathed through the hail of bullets and bombs. After the attack was over, military personnel salvaged whatever could be re-used to get as many surviving planes back into combat-ready condition should the Japanese return. Rumors ran rampant through the day, including one that an enemy invasion force had been sighted south of Oahu; another rumor was that Japanese paratroops had landed on the island wearing blue uniforms.

OPPOSITE: In this aerial photograph of the Navy Yard's dry docks, taken on December 10, 1941, the damaged battleship *Pennsylvania* and the ruined destroyers *Cassin* and *Downes* sit in the dock at the bottom. Above them, the torpedoed cruiser *Helena* awaits temporary patchwork before heading to California's Mare Island Navy Yard for more extensive repairs. At the top of the photograph, all that can be seen afloat of the destroyer *Shaw* is her after section. The waters are streaked with fuel oil leaking from the sunken ships of Battleship Row.

ABOVE: A ground-crew mechanic inspects the charred remains of a Curtiss P-40 to see what can be salvaged. All told, eighty-three of 153 fighter and reconnaissance planes based at Wheeler Field were destroyed or knocked out of commission. During the nearly two-hour attack, only fourteen U.S. Army pilots managed to take off to oppose the enemy. The only ones to get their fighters in the air successfully were from the squadrons based at the training field at Haleiwa.

ABOVE: The wreckage of a Curtiss P-40 Warhawk fighter plane stands at Bellows Field. A small airbase used primarily for training, Bellows was located on a stretch of white coral sand along the southeast coast of Oahu. A squadron of twelve P-40s had flown in on December 6 for gunnery practice. The following morning, nine Zeros strafed the planes parked on the runway. Lieutenant Hans C. Christiansen was killed as he climbed into the cockpit of his P-40. Two other pilots, Second Lieutenant George A. Whitman and First Lieutenant Samuel W. Bishop, also attempted to take off. Whitman managed to get airborne with two Zeros on his tail, but was hit and killed fifty feet (15.2m) off the ground, sending the P-40 crashing onto the beach. Taking off seconds behind Whitman, Bishop could not gain altitude and was also shot down, his plane crashing into the ocean about a half mile (.8m) from shore. Despite a leg wound, Bishop managed to swim to shore, his Mae West life jacket keeping him afloat. Each pilot was awarded the Silver Star for bravery.

BELOW: In the shallow waters off Kaneohe Bay Naval Air Station, the body of an unidentified sailor washes ashore. A victim of the Japanese strafing attack that morning, he was one of the 2,340 servicemen killed in action on December 7, 1941. The U.S. Navy lost 2,107 officers and enlisted personnel, while the U.S. Army and Army Air Force suffered 233 fatalities.

ABOVE: As soon as the attack had ended at Wheeler Field, the wreckage of demolished aircraft was bulldozed into piles of useless junk to clear the flight line for operations. Prior to the attack, as headquarters had ordered, the planes were parked wingtip to wingtip at ten- to fifteen-foot (3–4.6m) intervals. While it was easier to guard the planes against any possible threat of fifth-column sabotage, it also made it easier for the Japanese to quickly destroy the U.S. Army pursuit planes and gain vital air superiority over the skies of Oahu.

LEFT: Aboard the *Oklahoma* (her hull is to the right), Electrician's Mate First Class Irvin H. Thesman was ironing a pair of dungarees when the P.A. system blared out: "Man your battle stations! This is no drill! No shit!" As he was rushing to his station in the aft steering compartment, he heard a loud "hrump" and felt the ship shake. He made it to his station, but was trapped inside with seven other men when the ship capsized. They were rescued the next day after thirty hours. As the ship rolled over on her port side, those who'd made it out on deck climbed over the starboard side and walked with the roll until the masts of the ship hit bottom. Seaman First Class Thomas Armstrong was among those who swam over to the *Maryland* (background); his watch had stopped at 0810. The lightly damaged *Maryland* was fully repaired and ready for duty in less than two weeks.

ABOVE: By the time this photo of Ford Island was taken, the fires at Hangar Six had been extinguished. The PBY Catalina seaplanes not damaged in the attack are here being readied for patrol in search of the enemy. Across the channel waters, the heavily damaged *Nevada* (top) has settled to the bottom of the shallow waters off Waipio Peninsula. Refloated and temporarily repaired by mid-April, the *Nevada* then sailed from Pearl Harbor to a West Coast navy yard for complete repairs and modernization. By December 1942, the *Nevada* rejoined the fleet, where she would serve with distinction in both the Atlantic and Pacific Theaters and earn seven Battle Stars for her service in World War II.

CHIEF WATERTENDER PETER TOMICH
United States Navy

★ ★ ★ ★

Peter Tomich, a native of Prolog, Austria, and already a twenty-year navy veteran, was topside when two torpedoes struck the *Utah*. When the order was given to abandon ship as it capsized, he rushed to his engineering plant duty station to secure the ship's boilers before they blew up. Before the ship turned completely over he also saw to it that all fire room personnel had managed to get out, but his devotion to duty cost him his life. The story does not end there. The telegram to his next of kin, informing them that Tomich had been killed and awarded the Medal of Honor, was returned "address unknown." Authorities were never able to locate any next of kin, and his medal has never been claimed. Since 1943, his medal has been displayed on a ship named for him, at various government buildings, and in naval museums. Several of Tomich's shipmates, survivors from the USS *Utah*, believe they may have found some distant relatives in Europe, but the saga of his unclaimed medal continues at this writing.

RIGHT: **When tapping was heard from the overturned hull of the *Utah* (center), a work detail was sent over to cut a hole in her bottom, freeing Fireman Second Class John B. Vaessen; he was the last survivor off the ship. Meanwhile, once the air assault on the *Raleigh* (right) had ended, the men turned to the task of keeping the cruiser from capsizing. Captain R.B. Simons, after securing pumps from the Navy Yard and nearby ships, gave orders to put both scout planes into the water and jettison all unnecessary topside weight. Plane catapults, cranes, ladders, anchors, lockers, torpedo tubes, life rafts—nearly everything the crew could pry loose—went over the side, lightening the stricken ship's load by more than sixty tons (54.4t). A yeoman with pencil and paper charted where the equipment was thrown into the water for later recovery. The efforts of Captain Simons and his crew ensured that the ship lived to fight another day.**

LEFT: The *Cassin* and *Downes* lie side by side in the dry dock, with the battleship *Pennsylvania* behind them. The two destroyers had been awaiting repairs when they were hit by "Val" dive-bombers. Fires consumed the ships as leaking fuel ignited and the stores of ammunition began to explode. After the order to abandon ship was given, Fireman First Class Edward Kwolik refused to leave, keeping a steady stream of water trained on the after engine room hatch until everyone got out from below decks. Later, to quench the fires, the dry dock was ordered flooded, and the *Cassin* floated free of her keel blocks, toppling onto the port side of the *Downes*. A makeshift fire-fighting team of sailors, marines, and civilian yard workers battled valiantly for more than two hours before all the fires were put out.

ABOVE: Initially, the *Cassin* (right) and *Downes* were written off as total losses. Their salvage was not a high priority, but the dock had to be cleared for other important ship work. To lighten the ships, much of the topside equipment, gun turrets, and superstructure had to be removed, and the ships were made watertight for re-floating. Their machinery was found to be in good shape, though the hulls were warped and bent beyond use. The navy decided to build new hulls and outfit them with the salvaged equipment. More than 560 crates of parts, weighing more than one thousand tons (900t) total, were shipped to the Mare Island Navy Yard. Later, the parts would be incorporated into the new hulls with the original thirty-seven-ton (33.3t) stern sections, which had been saved with their nameplates carefully preserved. By February 1944, both ships were back in full service.

LEFT: The fires on the *Arizona* (left) would burn and smolder for three days before they were finally extinguished. When it was safe, work parties went aboard to remove as many of the 1,177 dead as possible. Of the 229 bodies recovered, only 105 men could be identified. Ahead of the *Arizona*, work is already under way to free the lightly damaged *Tennessee* (right), which was wedged against the mooring quay when the *West Virginia* (center) sank.

At sunset on December 7, an exhausted Ensign Edmond M. Jacoby was relieved from fire-fighting duties on the *West Virginia*. As he started walking toward Ford Island's Bachelors Officers' Quarters for a sandwich, a bugle sounded evening colors. Jacoby snapped to attention and saluted.

FOLLOWING PAGES: As part of salvage operations, a crew inspected the *Arizona* to determine if the bodies of more than 900 men still aboard could be feasibly removed. In 1948, a nine-man Graves Registration board decided to leave the remaining bodies aboard, concluding that the operation was too difficult and dangerous and that it would be better to let the battleship and crew remain where they lay. In the short time they lived after the attack, these men fought and died for the *Arizona*; it seemed only right that they stay with their ship.

LIEUTENANT COMMANDER SAMUEL GLENN FUQUA
United States Navy

As the senior officer to survive the *Arizona's* devastating explosion, Lieutenant Commander Samuel Fuqua won the Congressional Medal of Honor for his direction of fire-fighting and rescue efforts. His citation describes his leadership on the ship's quarterdeck, where he had initially been knocked out by the explosion of one of the first bombs: "Upon regaining consciousness, he began to direct the fighting of the fire and the rescue of wounded personnel. Almost immediately, there was a tremendous explosion forward.... The whole forward part of the ship was enveloped in flames that spread rapidly. Wounded and burned men poured out of the ship to the quarterdeck. Despite these conditions...Lt. Cmdr. Fuqua...supervised the rescue of these men in such an amazingly calm and cool manner and with such excellent judgement that it inspired everyone that saw him and undoubtedly resulted in saving many lives. After realizing the ship could not be saved..., he gave the order to abandon ship. He continued to remain on the quarterdeck and direct the abandoning ship and rescue of personnel until satisfied that all personnel that could be had been saved, after which he left his ship with the last boatload."

RIGHT: **Like a stranded whale, the capsized hull of the *Oklahoma* lolls on Battleship Row. When the ship began heeling over, the lights went out and the men below decks, who had been racing for battle stations, found themselves in a battle to survive with just the flickering light of emergency lamps. They maneuvered towards the air pockets of the compartments they had become trapped in and tapped on the hull. To cut through the ship's bottom, a rescue team of civilian workers, led by Julio DeCastro, was brought over from the Navy Yard with pneumatic equipment. Joe Bulga, a strapping twenty-one-year-old Hawaiian, worked tirelessly, opening bulkhead after bulkhead into compartments deep inside the hull. He reached eight men in one compartment, but after being soaked and trapped for nearly thirty hours, they wcrc hardly able to move. One by one, Bulga lifted each man up through the hatch, where other workers pulled them to safety. Bulga, DeCastro, and eighteen other men from Shop 11 were awarded Navy citations "for their heroic work with utter disregard for their own safety."**

RIGHT TOP: **Before removing the powder casings, this clean-up worker adjusts a pump in the 14-inch (35.6cm) magazine of the *Oklahoma*. The cleaning crews had to work in difficult, unpleasant, and often dangerous conditions. All compartments, decks, bulkheads, ammunition, equipment, stores—everything below the surface in the sunken ships—was covered with a heavy coat of the oil that had spilled into the harbor from the ruptured fuel tanks. Each man of the cleaning gang wore a special tank suit and knee-high rubber boots.**

RIGHT BOTTOM: **Conditions in the murky waters of Pearl Harbor were extremely poor, and without competent divers, the salvage work would have been impossible. Even with powerful lights, visibility was barely one to two feet (0.3–0.6m), and working underwater in the ships' tight compartments, many of them upside-down, was disorienting. More than five thousand dives, for a total of more than twenty thousand man-hours underwater, were made by U.S. Navy and civilian divers. Throughout the salvage efforts, there was only one casualty, a remarkable record considering the many hazards involved.**

ABOVE: During salvage operations, the *Oklahoma* emerges after eighteen months underwater. When the attack hit, Marine Sergeant Thomas E. Hailey, a twenty-five-year-old from St. Joseph, Missouri, never made it to the 5-inch (12.7cm) anti-aircraft gun station pictured here. Asleep in his quarters on the *Oklahoma's* third deck, Hailey sprang from his bunk at the call to battle stations. He sprinted for his topside station in his underwear, feeling the thuds of the torpedoes as he scrambled. Before he reached his post, the ship began to roll over. Hailey made it into the water and swam to the *Maryland*, some thirty feet (9.1m) away. Thrashing wildly to push back oil that had spewed from his stricken ship, he made it to a rope hanging from the ship's side. After pulling several of his shipmates aboard, he spied a 5-inch gun not fully manned. He rallied some dripping and oil-soaked sailors from the *Oklahoma* and brought the gun into action.

RIGHT: To bring the *Oklahoma* back to an even keel during salvage operations, it was necessary to remove as much weight as possible. Nearly 400,000 gallons (1,514,000L) of fuel oil were removed with steam-driven pumps. About one third of the ammunition and powder casings, exclusive of the 14-inch (35.6cm) shells, were also removed. As submerged compartments became accessible, mud and seawater was pumped out and then the compartments were made airtight. Here, the *Oklahoma's* aft 14-inch gun turrets are covered with sea growth as they come to the surface in March 1943. The guns would be removed when the ship was righted. In this view, the ship is tilted 34 degrees from center.

ABOVE: The *Oklahoma* was slowly turned over by an array of twenty-one large winches anchored on the shore of Ford Island. Steel cables ran from the winches to huge forty-foot (12.1m) struts welded onto the hull, slowly pulling the ship to an upright position. Efforts to raise the ship began on March 8, 1943, and the job was done by mid-June. The recovery of nearly four hundred bodies proved a difficult task. Three hundred and eighty-four could not be identified and are buried at Honolulu's Punchbowl National Cemetery in common graves marked "Unknown: December 7, 1941." Twenty-one officers and 386 enlisted men were killed in action on the Oklahoma and twenty-six were wounded.

BELOW: **A barnacle-encrusted hulk with nearly all its superstructure removed is all that remains of the once-mighty battleship *Oklahoma*. In one of the biggest and most difficult salvage operations in U.S. Navy history, she was finally righted and re-floated in November 1943. After she was patched up and temporarily repaired, it was decided that her restoration was impractical. She was sold in 1947 for scrap to Moore Drydock Co. of Oakland, California. She denied the scrappers their due, though, when she sank 540 miles (864km) northwest of Oahu while in tow for the West Coast. Perhaps at 3,000 fathoms (5,490m) beneath the Pacific, she found a more appropriate end for a warrior.**

ABOVE: **The *Oklahoma* was considered too badly damaged to restore, but the derelict hulk had to be removed from the harbor to make room for other ships. Confronted with so formidable a task, the U.S. Navy Salvage Division contracted the Pacific Bridge Company to help. It was decided that the destroyed *Oklahoma* should first be righted and then re-floated. In the end, righting and floating the *Oklahoma* took two years; patching her up took another eight months to complete.**

ABOVE: The *Shaw* was originally reported as a total loss, but its machinery turned out to be in good condition. Only the area from the bridge to the bow was severely damaged. After the forward part was cut away at the Navy Yard, a false bow was fabricated in the Pearl Harbor shops and installed. A temporary mast and a steering-control station aft were also added. Following trials to test her for seaworthiness, the *Shaw* departed Pearl Harbor on February 9, 1942, under the command of Commander W.G. Jones, for an extensive rebuilding at the Mare Island Navy Yard. The first of the severely damaged ships to put to sea, the *Shaw* would serve with distinction throughout World War II, earning eleven battle stars for action in, among others, the Battle of the Santa Cruz Islands, Guadalcanal, Leyte Operations, and the Southern Philippines.

RIGHT: After the attack, the sunken battleship *West Virginia* was thought to be a total loss as a result of the devastating torpedo damage that had opened up her port side. Like a ghost reappearing from the dead, the battleship was raised from the murky bottom of Pearl Harbor thanks to the ingenuity and resolve of the U.S. Navy Salvage Division. Here, the ship is being moved by navy tugs from the dry dock, after temporary repairs, to an outfitting pier where she will be made ready for a voyage to the West Coast of the United States for a complete modernization. The newly rebuilt ship returned to active duty in October 1944, in time to participate in the Philippine, Iwo Jima, and Okinawa campaigns of the Pacific war.

On September 2, 1945, the *West Virginia* was anchored near the battleship *Missouri* in Tokyo Bay to witness the surrender of Japan. The *West Virginia* was the only battleship present that bore the scars of December 7, 1941. An old score had finally been settled.

OPPOSITE: **The shattered, sunken ships of Battleship Row are seen in this aerial view, taken three days after the attack. All the fires have been extinguished and salvage work is in its early stages. Most of the fuel oil in the ships was pumped out when possible, but unrecovered oil continued to leak from the torn hulls, polluting the waters of the harbor for months. In the upper left portion of the photograph, the *California* sits on the bottom of the harbor. In the center is the overturned hull of the *Oklahoma*, next to the *Maryland*, followed by the sunken *West Virginia*, alongside the *Tennessee*. The remains of the *Arizona* can be seen to the lower right. All the ships in this view, except for the *Oklahoma* and *Arizona*, would return to active service.**

LEFT: **On the Sunday morning of the assault, Honolulu residents did not at first comprehend what was happening. Even when they heard the bombs and saw the smoke rising from the direction of Pearl Harbor and Hickam Field, most believed they were seeing U.S. military training exercises. Unfortunately, the civilian inhabitants of the island were not to be spared the devastating touch of war's hand.**

Boxer Toy Tamanaha, a native Hawaiian, a contender for the flyweight championship, paid no attention to the sound of the bombardment, thinking it was only more war games. He had stopped at the Cherry Blossom Sweet Shop for a popsicle when the shop exploded, throwing Tamanaha into the street. He was conscious for a moment and saw that his legs were badly mangled, then he passed out. When he awoke in the hospital, his legs had been amputated to save his life.

The explosion, like nearly all those that occurred in downtown Honolulu, was caused by U.S. Navy anti-aircraft shells. In the heat of battle, some gunners improperly set fuses, which consequently failed to function in the air and exploded on contact with the ground instead.

BELOW: After the attack began, the Lunalilo School was set up as a Red Cross aid station and was attending to early casualties when the nurses and their patients were forced to evacuate the school. Flaming debris from a nearby fire had been carried by the tradewinds, setting the school ablaze.

Earlier that morning, Tsuneko Ogure had been looking forward to the University of Hawaii's sophomore picnic, scheduled for that afternoon, where she planned to see her friend, a seventeen-year-old army private from her creative writing class. They both dreamed of one day writing the "great American novel." Tsuneko never wrote her book (though she did become a journalist), but James Jones, the young soldier, did. The book was *From Here To Eternity*.

ABOVE: On the morning of December 7, midway through the attack, Kaneohe residents Joseph K. Adams, his son John, and a neighbor—all three employees at the Navy Yard—heard the summons over the radio for all workers to report to work immediately. They got in Joe's green 1937 Packard and sped off. They were on Judd Street in Honolulu, about halfway to the yard from their homes, when an errant anti-aircraft shell exploded near the car, sending shrapnel ripping through the car, killing the three men instantly.

More shrapnel from the same explosion went hurtling across the street, fatally wounding twelve-year-old Matilda K. Faufat, who was standing in a doorway. She died before she even made it to the operating table.

ABOVE: **Another errant shell struck a building at King and McCully Streets, causing it to erupt into flames, which quickly spread through the block of stores and dwellings. It was the worst fire in the city of Honolulu that day. Thirteen buildings were completely destroyed, and thirty-one families lost their homes.**

Hayako Ohata, her baby daughter, and her aunt were killed in the explosion. Little three-month-old Janet Y. Ohata was the youngest person to die in the attack, which claimed the lives of forty-eight civilians, including twelve children. Another 225 citizens were treated for wounds.

ABOVE: This "Val" dive-bomber, one of fifteen the Japanese lost during the attack, was shot down by the *Nevada* and crashed near Pearl City. For the most part, the suddenness of the attack made countermeasures difficult. When general quarters sounded aboard the destroyer USS *Chew*, Fireman Second Class Jesse Pond arrived at his 3-inch (7.6cm) anti-aircraft gun post to find he was the only member of his gun crew aboard. With the others ashore, Pond enlisted volunteers from the engine room, giving them a quick run-through on how to work the gun. Fireman Second Class Art Clymer learned how to load, Machinist's Mate Third Class Jules Schoenberg to train and fire the weapon, and Fireman Third Class "Red" Grossman to remove the hot shells. Fireman Third Class Dave Taylor put on the headphones to keep in contact with the bridge. Ready in less than ten minutes, the new gun crew began firing at the attackers and later scored a direct hit on a "Val."

BELOW: **During a strafing run at Hickam Field, this low-flying Zero was downed by defensive ground fire and crashed at nearby Fort Kam, hitting a palm tree and killing four men on the base. The aircraft, a Mitsubishi A6M2 Zero from the *Akagi*, was flown by Petty Officer First Class Takeshi Hirano, who most likely was killed before his plane hit the ground. At the time, the U.S. Army knew little of this new Japanese fighter plane, and the wreckage was secured and shipped to the Lockheed Aircraft Co. in Burbank, California, for restoration and evaluation. For the remainder of the war, Hirano's Zero was paraded in War Bond Drives throughout the United States.**

ABOVE: **The recovered wreckage of a torpedo bomber is being lifted out of the water. The pilot was Lieutenant Mimori Suzuki, from the carrier *Kaga*. As his plane flew over Southeast Loch to make his torpedo run at about forty to fifty feet (12.2–15.2m) off the water, he was shot down by Chief Gunner's Mate Harry L. Skinner, of the destroyer USS *Bagley*. The plane crashed off the Officers' Club landing, killing Suzuki and his two crewmen. The *Bagley*, docked in the area just outside of the Navy Yard, was in a perfect position to fire at the torpedo bombers as they attacked Battleship Row. *Bagley*'s machine-gunners claimed to have shot down five planes that morning.**

ABOVE: **Several days after the attack, the charred and partially decomposed body of a Japanese flier is recovered from the harbor, where he crashed when his plane was shot down. Fifteen of the twenty-nine aircraft lost in the raid by the Japanese were from the carrier _Kaga_. She lost four Zero fighters, five "Kate" bombers, six "Val" dive-bombers, and all thirty-one of the air crew in those planes.**

LEFT: **Lieutenant Fusata Iida, in a grave near but separate from the American dead, is accorded a military burial with honors, customarily given to officers. At about 0900 on December 7, Iida led a squadron of nine Zeros from the *Soryu* in a second strike on Kaneohe Naval Air Station. Hit by ground fire, Iida's fighter began streaming fuel. The squadron leader realized he could not make it back and signaled for the others to return to the carriers. That morning before takeoff, Iida had told his comrades that if he could not return, he would crash his plane into an enemy target. So he banked back and flew for the Kaneohe armory. As he dove down, though, Iida fell under fire from machine guns and was fatally hit. His plane crashed into a hill, skidded across, and piled up on an embankment.**

ABOVE LEFT AND RIGHT: **In these photographs, it is nearly twenty-four hours after the planes of the Japanese Strike Force left the scene of their great victory. The sound of thundering explosions and the fury of battle have faded away, leaving an uneasy quiet. The time has come for the defenders and inhabitants of Oahu to regroup, heal the wounded, and begin burying the dead.**

In the hills overlooking Kaneohe Bay, the skies are gray and overcast. A burial detail (left) is placing the coffins of the fifteen officers and enlisted personnel killed in action at the Naval Air Station into a temporary common grave bulldozed in the sand dunes. The marine honor guard presents arms as the funeral service begins, the flag the fifteen men had died for draped over the coffins (right).

OPPOSITE: **The detail snaps to attention as the chaplain, with Bible in hand (upper left), steps forward to say a few final words and lead the men in prayer for their fallen comrades. Then a squad of marines steps forward to render honors by firing three rifle volleys (upper right) over the grave. The grave has been covered over as the men stand at attention to give the final salute (right) to their shipmates. A bugler at the head of the grave begins playing "Taps," the mournful tune echoing across the sandy hillside.**

Similar ceremonies would take place in the next few days at other cemeteries on the island as hundreds of victims of the onslaught were laid to rest. About 330 navy dead were buried at Honolulu's Oahu Cemetery and another 204 were interred at Red Hill Cemetery. The army buried their casualties at the Schofield Barracks post cemetery. After the war ended, many of the victims were shipped to the United States to be re-interred in family plots or national cemeteries. Another 333 bodies were moved to the Punchbowl National Cemetery, where the names of 1,608 men were placed on the walls of the Court of the Missing.

THE END OF THE BEGINNING

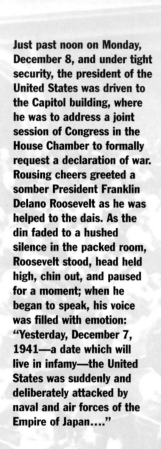

Just past noon on Monday, December 8, and under tight security, the president of the United States was driven to the Capitol building, where he was to address a joint session of Congress in the House Chamber to formally request a declaration of war. Rousing cheers greeted a somber President Franklin Delano Roosevelt as he was helped to the dais. As the din faded to a hushed silence in the packed room, Roosevelt stood, head held high, chin out, and paused for a moment; when he began to speak, his voice was filled with emotion: "Yesterday, December 7, 1941—a date which will live in infamy—the United States was suddenly and deliberately attacked by naval and air forces of the Empire of Japan...."

The day after the attack, amid the extensive clean-up and repair work on ships and stations on Oahu, Admiral Kimmel issued the following message of encouragement to all hands: "From CinCPac [Commander-in-Chief, Pacific Fleet, Kimmel's title]: Your conduct and action have been splendid. We took a blow yesterday (Sunday). It will not be a short war. We will give many heavy blows to the Japanese. While you have suffered from a treacherous attack, your Commander-in-Chief has informed me that your courage and stamina remain magnificent. You know you will have your revenge. Recruiting stations are jammed with men eager to join you. Carry on."

Elsewhere in the United States, shock and sorrow gave way to resolve. The Japanese, believing that their early victories would sap American morale, had grossly underestimated the willingness of the American people to pull together swiftly on the battlefront and at home to wage a successful counteroffensive. They were also mistaken in their belief that the strong Isolationist movement in the U.S. against participation in foreign wars would hasten the U.S. to seek an armistice or truce to bring the war to a quick conclusion. When Admiral Yamamoto learned that Japan's ultimatum had been delivered an hour after the attack had begun, he said, "I fear all we have done is to awaken a sleeping giant and fill him with a great resolve."

The cry "Remember Pearl Harbor!" would echo across the battlefields of the Pacific until the war officially came to an end (on the decks of the battleship Missouri, in Tokyo Bay) with the surrender of Japan on September 2, 1945.

When the last planes of the Japanese strike force departed the scene of the carnage they had wrought at Pearl Harbor, it marked the end of the beginning of America's entry into World War II. It also marked the beginning of the end of the Empire of Japan.

LEFT: **President Roosevelt ended his emotionally charged speech by saying, "I ask that the Congress declare that since the unprovoked and dastardly attack by Japan on Sunday, December 7, a state of war exists between the United States and the Empire of Japan." The address had lasted fewer than six minutes, but it ended in a ten-minute standing ovation. The vote was 420-to-1 in favor of war, the lone dissenting vote cast by Representative Jeanette Rankin of Montana, a longtime member of the House who had also cast the only "nay" vote against the war in 1917.**

BELOW: **Early that morning around the country, long lines of patriotic volunteers formed at recruiting stations to enlist to avenge the attack on Pearl Harbor. Here, a mother hangs a red and white banner with a blue star in the window of her home. Each blue star represented a member of the family in the armed forces; a gold star meant that one of them had paid the full measure.**

OPPOSITE: **On street corners across the country, newsboys were shouting, "Extra! Extra! Read all about it! Japan declares war!" People flocked to local newsstands, eager to read the latest news, or huddled around their radios, listening for the latest bulletins.**

December 7 in the United States found some people going to church, while for others it was another workday. Many spent a leisurely Sunday morning at home reading the comics, while others attended football games or concerts. Others may have planned on going to a movie or to visit relatives. Regardless of people's mundane pursuits, word of the surprise attack in Hawaii spread quickly throughout the nation.

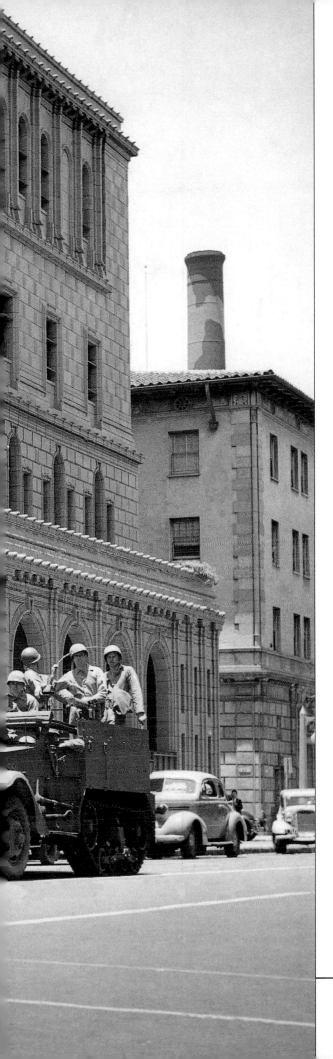

LEFT: **A column of U.S. Army light tanks rumble through a street in downtown Honolulu, symbols of the new state of affairs on the island. Shortly after noon on December 7, General Walter C. Short had met with the Governor of Hawaii, Joseph B. Poindexter, to place the island under martial law.**

As soon as martial law was declared, the FBI and U.S. Army Intelligence arrested 370 Japanese, ninety-eight German, and fourteen Italian residents. With martial law also came curfews, blackouts, military control of the courts, gas rationing, food rationing, censorship of mail and news releases, prohibition of the sale of alcohol to the Japanese population, and countless other privations. In addition, a number of publications were discontinued, especially those owned or controlled by Japanese. Martial law lasted nearly three years and was finally abolished on October 24, 1944.

ABOVE: **A Japanese two-man midget submarine is on display in New York City's Times Square for a war bond rally, May 2, 1943. Due to gyroscope and engine problems, the sub had failed in its attempt to enter Pearl Harbor, drifting onto a reef off Bellows Field, where it was recovered on December 8, 1941 (see page 34). One crewman perished in the surf and the other, Ensign Kazuo Sakamaki, was captured when he washed up on the shore, becoming Japanese prisoner of war number one. The submarine was refurbished and shipped to the mainland in mid-1942. The sub was taken on a forty-one-state tour across the United States to promote the sale of War Bonds, which raised millions of dollars during the war. This very sub is currently on display at the Admiral Nimitz Museum and Historical Center in Fredericksburg Texas.**

LEFT: **Clearly visible just below the surface of Pearl Harbor's waters are the sunken remains of the battleship *Arizona*. In March 1950, Admiral Arthur Radford ordered a flagpole mounted on the hulk and a temporary platform built to accommodate visitors and ceremonies. Although the ship was no longer in commission, Radford ordered that a detail of Navymen raise the colors each morning and lower them at sunset, a practice that is still carried on today.**

In 1961, Congress authorized money to build a permanent memorial to the *Arizona*. Supplementing this fund were additional monies raised through private subscription and donation, as well as by less conventional means. On the night of March 25, 1961, Elvis Presley gave a benefit performance at Pearl Harbor's Bloch Arena, and the proceeds from the concert, $64,696.73, were donated to the building fund for the memorial. Officially dedicated on Memorial Day, 1962, the graceful structure that is the USS *Arizona* Memorial spans the wreck of the once-proud vessel without actually touching any part of the ship itself.

ABOVE: **Secretary of the Navy Frank Knox (seated at the desk) held a press conference on December 15, 1941, after coming back from a hurried inspection trip to Pearl Harbor. Having determined firsthand the extent of the damage, he had returned the day before and reported his findings directly to President Roosevelt. Secretary Knox had a graphic story to relate, though for security reasons it was not entirely complete. Knox told the reporters about the ships that had been sunk and damaged as well as about the heavy loss of life. He also acknowledged that the attack had been a surprise to everyone concerned.**

FOLLOWING PAGES: **Visitors to the elegant white, chapel-like memorial that straddles the *Arizona* arrive by boat. After disembarking, they enter through the museum room, which contains mementos of the ship, eventually moving on to the assembly area, with its open portals through which the visitors can look down at the rusting hull of the ship. About every 30 seconds, one or two droplets of oil the size of a small coin or marble rise up from the section of the hull near the flagpole. Some tour guides compare the oil droplets to the tears of the dead sailors or say that the ship still bleeds for her crew. At the far end of the memorial is the shrine room, where on a large wall of Vermont marble the names of the 1,177 men who lost their lives on the *Arizona* are engraved. Many people who visit pause to reflect about the events that occurred at that site all those decades ago. Some feel a moment of sadness mixed with pride, some feel pain or anger or even love, but everyone leaves humbled by the experience. The memorial provides a dramatic setting in which to honor the fallen and to "Remember Pearl Harbor."**

APPENDIX

Ships Named for Pearl Harbor Heroes

DD = Destroyer   DE = Destroyer Escort   DDG = Guided Missile Destroyer
APD = Destroyer Transport   FF = Frigate

Austin DE-15	John A. Austin, Chief Carpenter	*Oklahoma*
Barber DE-161	Malcom Barber, Fireman 2/c	*Oklahoma*
	Randolph Barber, Fireman 2/c	
	Leroy Barber, Fireman 2/c	
Bates DE-68	Edward M. Bates, Ensign	*Arizona*
Bennion DD-662	Marvin Sharp Bennion, Captain	*West Virginia*
Booth DE-170	Robert Sinclair Booth, Ensign	*Arizona*
Bowers DE-637	Robert Keith Bowers, Ensign	*California*
Buckley DE-51	John D. Buckley, Aviation Ordnanceman 3/c	*NAS Kaneohe Bay*
Charles Lawrence DE-53	Charles Lawrence, AMM2/c	*NAS Kaneohe Bay*
Christopher DE-100	Harold J. Christopher, Ensign	*Nevada*
Connoly DE-306	John Gaynor Connoly, Chief Pay Clerk	*Oklahoma*
Crowley DE-303	Thomas E. Crowley, Lt. Commander	*Arizona*
Darby DE-218	Marshall Eugene Darby, Jr., Ensign	*Oklahoma*
Day DE-225	Francis Daniel Day, Chief Watertender	*Oklahoma*
Daniel T. *Griffin* DE-54	Daniel T. Griffin, AMM1/c	*NAS Kaneohe Bay*
Edward C. Daly DE-17	Edward C. Daly, Coxswain	*Downes*
Emery DE-28	Jack Mandeville Emery, Ensign	*Arizona*
England DE-635	John Charles England, Ensign	*Oklahoma*
Finnegan DE-303	William Michael Finnegan, Ensign	*Oklahoma*
Flaherty DE-135	Francis Charles Flaherty, Ensign	*Oklahoma*
Formoe DE-509	Clarence Melvin Formoe, AMM1/c	*NAS Kanehoe Bay*
Foss DE-59	Rodney Sheldon Foss, Ensign	*NAS Kanehoe Bay*
Fredrick C. Davis DE-136	Fredrick C. Davis, Ensign	*Nevada*
Gantner DE-60	Samual Merritt Gantner, Boatswain's Mate 2/c	*Nevada*
George W. Ingram DE-62	George W. Ingram, Seaman 2/c	*NAS Kaneohe Bay*
Gosselin APD-126	Edward Webb Gosselin, Ensign	*Arizona*
Halloran DE-305	William Ignatius Halloran, Ensign	*Arizona*
Haverson DE-316	Harold Aloysius Haverson, Lieutenant (jg)	*Utah*
Haverfield DE-393	James Wallace Haverfield, Ensign	*Arizona*
Herbert C. Jones DE-137	Herbert Charpiot Jones, Ensign	*California*
Hill DE-141	Edwin Joseph Hill, Chief Boatswain	*Nevada*
Hollis DE-794	Ralph Hollis, Ensign	*Arizona*
Howard D. Crow DE-252	Howard Daniel Crow, Ensign	*Maryland*
Ira Jeffery DE-63	Ira Well Jeffery, Ensign	*California*
James E. Craig DE-201	James Edwin Craig, Lt. Commander	*Pennsylvania*
Jordan DE-204	Julian Bethane Jordan, Lieutenant	*Oklahoma*
J. Richard Ward DE-243	James Richard Ward, Seaman 1/c	*Oklahoma*
Kidd DD-661	Isaac Campbell Kidd, Rear Admiral	*Arizona*
Kirkpatrick DE-318	Thomas L. Kirkpatrick, Captain	*Arizona*
Lake DE-301	John Ervin Lake, Jr. Pay Clerk	*Arizona*
Lamons DE-743	Kenneth Tafe Lamons, Boatswain's Mate 2/c	*Nevada*
Lee Fox DE-65	Lee Fox, Jr., Ensign	*NAS Kaneohe Bay*
Leopold DE-319	Robert Lawrence Leopold, Ensign	*Arizona*
Manlove DE-36	Arthur Cleon Manlove, Electrician	*Arizona*
Manning DE-199	Milburn A. Manning, AMM3/c	*NAS Kaneohe Bay*
Marsh DE-699	Benjamin Raymond Marsh, Jr., Ensign	*Arizona*
McClelland DE-750	Thomas Alfred McClelland, Ensign	*West Virginia*
Menges DE-320	Herbert Hugo Menges, Ensign	*Enterprise*
Merrill DE-392	Howard Deel Merrill, Ensign	*Arizona*
Miller FF-1091	Doris Miller, Mess Attendent 2/c	*West Virginia*
Moore DE-240	Fred Kenneth Moore, Seaman 1/c	*Arizona*
Neuendorf DE-200	William Frederich Neuendorf, Jr., Seaman 1/c	*Nevada*
Newman DE=205	Laxto Gail Newman, AMM3/c	*NAS Kaneohe Bay*
O'Niell DE-188	William Thomas O'Niell, Ensign	*Arizona*
Otterstetter DE-244	Carl William Otterstetter, Seaman 2/ c	*NAS Kaneohe Bay*
Pharris FF-1094	Jackson C. Pharris, Gunner	*California*
Pride DE-323	Lewis Bailey Pride, Jr.	*Oklahoma*
Rall DE-304	Richard Redner Rall, Lieutenant (jg) Marine Corps	*Pennsylvania*
Reeves DE-156	Thomas James Reeves, Chief Radioman	*California*
Register APD-92	Paul James Register, Lt. Commander	*Arizona*
Richey DE-385	Joseph Lee Richey, Ensign	*California*
Ross DDG-70	Donald K. Ross, Machinist	*Nevada*
Sanders DE-40	Eugene Thomas Sanders, Chief Boatswain	*Arizona*
Schmitt DE-676	Aloysius H. Schmitt, Lieutenant (jg), Chaplain	*Oklahoma*
Scott DE-214	Robert R. Scott, Machinist Mate 1/c	*California*
Sederstrom DE-31	Delmore Sederstrom, Ensign	*Oklahoma*
Smartt DE-257	Joseph G. Smartt, Ensign	*NAS Kaneohe Bay*
Solar DE-221	Adolfo Solar, Boatswain's Mate 1/c	*Nevada*
Stern DE-187	Charles M. Stern, Jr., Ensign	*Oklahoma*
Stockdale DE-399	Lewis Stevens Stockdale, Ensign	*Oklahoma*
Thomas J. Gary DE-326	Thomas Jones Gary, Seaman 2/c	*California*
Tomich DE-242	Peter Tomich, Chief Watertender	*Utah*
Uhlmann DD-687	Robert William Uhlmann, Ensign	*NAS Kaneohe Bay*
Van Valkenburg DD-656	Franklin Van Valkengurg, Captain	*Arizona*
Walter S. Brown DE-258	Walter Scott Brown, AMM2/c	*NAS Kaneohe Bay*
Weaver DE-741	Luther Dayton Weaver, Seaman 1/c	*NAS Kaneohe Bay*
William C. Miller DE-259	William Cicero Miller, Radioman 3/c	*Enterprise*
Willis DE-395	Walter Michael Willis, Ensign	*Enterprise*
Wyman DE-38	Eldon P. Wyman, Ensign	*Oklahoma*

U.S. Ships at Pearl Harbor Lost During World War Two

Ship	Date
Arizona BB-39	Dec. 7, 1941
Blue DD-387	Aug. 23, 1942
Gamble DM-15	Feb. 18, 1945
Grebe AM-43	Jan. 2, 1943
Helena CL-50	July 2, 1943
Henley DD-391	Oct. 3, 1943
Hull DD-350	Dec. 18, 1944
Jarvis DD-393	Aug. 9, 1942
Monaghan DD-354	Dec. 18, 1944
Neosho AO-23	May 11, 1942
Oklahoma BB-37	Dec. 7, 1941
Perry DMS-17	Sept. 13, 1944
Reid DD-369	Dec. 11, 1944
Thornton AVD-11	May 2, 1945
Tucker DD-374	Aug. 2, 1944
Utah AG-16	Dec. 7, 1941
Ward DD139	Dec. 7, 1944
Wasmuth DMS-15	Dec. 29, 1942
Worden DD-352	Jan. 12, 1943
PT-22	June 11, 1943
PT-28	Jan. 12, 1943

Note: See map on page 20 for explanation of ship designations

U.S. Casualties December 7, 1941

	KILLED	WOUNDED
Navy	1998	710
Army	233	364
Marines	109	69
Civilians	48	225
Totals	**2388**	**1368**

U.S. Aircraft Losses

	LOST	DAMAGED
Navy	92	31
Army	96	128
Totals	**169**	**159**

Damage to United States Navy Ships

SHIP	REMARKS	DATE rejoined fleet
Battleships		
Arizona BB-39	Sunk, total loss, on bottom at Pearl Harbor	
California BB-44	Sunk, raised, repaired, modernized	May 1944
Maryland BB-47	Moderately damaged, repaired	Feb. 1942
Nevada BB-36	Heavily damaged, re-floated, repaired, modernized	Dec. 1942
Oklahoma BB-37	Capsized, total loss, raised, lost at sea under tow to scrap yard	
Pennsylvania BB-38	Moderately damaged, repaired	Mar. 1941
Tennessee BB-43	Moderately damaged, repaired	Mar. 1942
West Virginia BB-48	Sunk, raised, repaired, modernized	July 1944
Cruisers		
Helena CL-50	Heavily damaged, repaired	June 1942
Honolulu CL-48	Damaged, repaired	Jan. 1942
Raleigh Cl-7	Heavily damaged, repaired, overhauled	July 1942
Destroyers		
Cassin DD-372	Heavily damaged, rebuilt	Feb. 1944
Downes DD-375	Heavily damaged, rebuilt	Nov. 1943
Helm DD-388	Damaged, repaired	Jan. 1942
Shaw DD373	Heavily damaged, rebuilt	June 1942
Minecraft		
Oglala CM-4	Sunk, raised, repaired	Feb. 1944
Auxiliaries		
Curtiss AV-4	Damaged, repaired	Jan. 1942
Sotoyomo YT-5	Sunk, raised, repaired	Aug. 1942
Utah AG-16	Capsized, total loss, on bottom at Pearl Harbor	
Vestal AR-4	Heavily damaged, re-floated, repaired	Feb. 1942
Floating dry dock	Sunk, raised, repaired	May 1942

Japanese Airmen Killed or Missing In Action During the Attack

AIRMEN	AIRCRAFT CARRIER	PLANE TYPE	ATTACK WAVE
Nagaaki Asahi	*Kaga*	D3A	II
Shunichi Atsumi	*Soryu*	A6M	II
Toshiaki Bando	*Kaga*	D3A	II
Hajime Goto	*Akagi*	D3A	II
Ippei Goto	*Kaga*	A6M	II
Toru Haneda	*Kaga*	A6M	II
Takeshi Hirano	*Akagi*	A6M	II
Fumio Hirashima	*Kaga*	D3A	II
Kinsuke Homma	*Akagi*	D3A	II
Fusata Iiida	*Soryu*	A6M	II
Fukumitsu Imai	*Kaga*	D3A	II
Tomio Inenaga	*Kaga*	A6M	II
Saburo Ishii	*Soryu*	A6M	II
Kunio Iwatsuki	*Shokaku*	D3A	I
Satoru Kawasaki	*Soryu*	D3A	II
Hirokichi Kinoshita	*Akagi*	D3A	II
Syuuuuzo Kitahara	*Kaga*	B5N	I
Isamu Kiyomura	*Hiryu*	D3A	II
Kenichi Kumamoto	*Kaga*	B5N	I
Tetsusaburo Kumazo	*Shokaku*	D3A	I
Hideyasu Kuwabara	*Soryu*	D3A	II
Kazuyoshi Kuwabata	*Kaga*	D3A	II
Yoshiharu Machimoto	*Kaga*	B5N	I
Saburo Makino	*Kaga*	D3A	II
Kenji Maruyama	*Soryu*	D3A	II
Yoshizo Masuda	*Kaga*	B5N	I
Isamu Matsuda	*Kaga*	B5N	I
Tsuneo Minamizaki	*Kaga*	D3A	II
Tsuneki Morita	*Kaga*	B4N	I
Hajime Murao	*Hiryu*	D3A	II
Izumi Nagai	*Kaga*	B5N	I
Shigenori Nishikaichi	*Hiryu*	A6M	II
Nafikatsu Ohashi	*Kaga*	B5N	I
Iwao Oka	*Kaga*	D3A	II
Shigenori Onikura	*Kaga*	B5N	II
Toshio Onishi	*Kaga*	B5N	I
Seiichi Ota	*Akagi*	D3A	II
Toshio Onishi	*Kaga*	B5N	I
Seiichi Ota	*Akagi*	D3A	II
Toshio Oyama	*Akagi*	D3A	II
Noboru Sakaguchi	*Kaga*	D3A	II
Kiyoshi Sakamoto	*Akagi*	D3A	II
Seinoshin Sano	*Kaga*	A6M	I
Chuji Shimakura	*Akagi*	D3A	II
Yoshio Shimizu	*Kaga*	B4N	I
Yoshio Shimizu	*Hiryu*	D3A	II
Koreyoshi Sotoyama	*Hiryu*	D3A	II
Shigeharu Sugaya	*Akagi*	B5N	I
Sueo Sukida	*Kaga*	D3A	II
Mitsumori Suzuki	*Kaga*	B5N	I
Ryochi Takahashi	*Soryu*	D3A	II
Hidemi Takeda	*Kaga*	B5N	I
Tomoharu Takeda	*Kaga*	B5N	I
Nobuo Tsuda	*Kaga*	D3A	II
Honetaro Ueda	*Kaga*	B5N	I
Nobuo Umezu	*Kaga*	B5N	I
Doshi Utsuki	*Akagi*	D3A	II

Japanese Ships Assigned to "Hawaii Operation"

TYPE	NAME		LOST
Aircraft Carriers	Akagi	June 5, 1942	Midway
	Kaga	June 4, 1942	Midway
	Shokaku	June 19, 1944	Philippine Sea
	Zuikaku	Oct. 25, 1944	Leyte Gulf
	Hiryu	June 5, 1942	Midway
	Soryu	June 4, 1942	Midway
Battleships	Hei	Nov. 13, 1942	Guadalcanal
	Kirishima	Nov. 15, 1942	Guadalcanal
Heavy Cruisers	Chikuma	Oct. 25, 1944	Leyte Gulf
	Tone	July 24, 1945	Kure
Light Cruisers	Abukuma	Oct. 27, 1944	Suriagao Strait
	Katori	Feb. 17, 1944	Tru
Destroyers	Akigumo	Apr. 11, 1944	Celebes Sea
	Arare	July 5, 1942	Aleutians
	Hamakaze	Apr. 7, 1945	S. of Kyushu
	Isokaze	Apr. 7, 1945	S. of Kyushu
	Kagero	May 8, 1943	Solomons
	Kasumi	Apr. 7, 1945	S. of Kyushu
	Sazanami	Jan. 14, 1944	Yap
	Shiranuhi	Oct. 27, 1944	Leyte gulf
	Tanikaze	June 9, 1944	Tawi Tawi
	Urakaze	Nov. 21, 1944	Formosa
	Ushio	Surrendered at Yokosuka Naval Base	
Oilers	Akebono Maru	March 30, 1944	Palau
	Kenyo Maru	Jan. 14, 1944	Palau
	Kokuyo Maru	July 30, 1944	Sulu Sea
	Kyokuto Maru	Sept. 21, 1944	Manila Harbor
	Nihon Maru	Jan. 14, 1944	Bismarks
	Shinkoku Maru	Feb. 17, 1944	Carolines
	Toei Maru	March 23, 1943	Makassar Strait
	Shirya	Sept. 21, 1943	N.E. Keelung
Submarines	There were 30 fleet submarines and five two-man midget submarines assigned to the Hawaii operation. All were sunk during the war except for the midget sub that was captured off Bellows Field on December 8, 1941.		

Information Courtesy of:
The Pearl Harbor History Associates, Inc.
P. O. Box 1007
Stratford, CT 06614

BIBLIOGRAPHY

Published Sources

Adams, Henry, H. *1942: The Year That Doomed the Axis*. New York: David McKay Co., Inc., 1967.

_____. *Years Of Deadly Peril: The Coming of the War 1939-1941*. New York: David McKay Co., Inc., 1969.

Allen, Gwenfread. *Hawaii's War Years*. Honolulu: University of Hawaii Press, 1950.

Altfeld, Bess. *The Pearl Harbor Collector's Series*. Mapmania Publishing Co., 1996.

Arakari, Leatrice R. and John R. Kuborn. *7 December 1941: The Air Force Story*. Hickam Airforce Base: Pacific Air Forces Office of History, 1991.

Blair, Clay. *Silent Victory: The U.S. Submarine War Against Japan*. Philadelphia: J. B. Lippencott Co., 1975.

Brown, Desoto. *Hawaii Goes To War*. Editions Limited, 1989.

Burlingame, Burl. *Advance Force: Pearl Harbor*. Kailua: Pacific Monograph, 1992.

Cohen, Stan. *East Wind Rain*. Pictorial Histories Publishing Co., 1991.

Cressman, Robert J. and J. Michael Wenger. *Infamous Day: Marines At Pearl Harbor 7 December 1941*. Government Printing Office,1992.

_____. *Steady Nerves and Stout Hearts*. Pictorial Histories Publishing Co., 1990.

Feis, Herbert. *The Road to Pearl Harbor*. Princeton: Princeton University Press, 1950.

Goldstein, Donald M., Katherine V. Dillon, and J. Michael Wenger. *Pearl Harbor: The Way it Was: The Original Photographs*. Brassey's, Inc., 1991.

Goodwin, Doris Kearns. *No Ordinary Time*. New York: Simon & Schuster, 1994.

Karig, Commander Walter, USN. *Battle Report: Pearl Harbor To Coral Sea*, Volume I. New York and Toronto: Farrar & Rhinehart,1944.

Kimmet, Larry and Margaret Regis. *The Attack On Pearl Harbor*. Navigator Press, 1991.

LaForte, Robert S. and Robert E. Marcello. *Remembering Pearl Harbor: Eyewitness Accounts by U.S. Military Men and Women*. Wilmington: Scholarly Resources, 1991.

Lord, Walter. *Day Of Infamy*. New York: Henry Holt Co., 1957.

Millis, Walter. *This Is Pearl! The United States and Japan—1941*. New York: William. Morrow & Co., 1947.

Morison, Samuel Elliot. *The Rising Sun in the Pacific: 1931-1942*. New York: Little, Brown & Co., 1957.

Mosley, Leonard. *Hirohito, Emperor of Japan*. Upper Saddle River: Prentice-Hall, Inc., 1966.

Parrish, Thomas. *Encyclopedia of World War II*. New York: Simon & Schuster, 1978.

Pond, Jesse E., Jr. *The Square Peg: A Tight Fit in a Tin Can*. Pearl Harbor History Associates, Inc., 1991.

Prange, Gordon W. with Donald M. Goldstein, and Katharine V. Dillon. *At Dawn We Slept*. New York: McGraw Hill, 1981.

_____. *December 7, 1941: The Day the Japanese Attacked Pearl Harbor*. New York: McGraw Hill, 1988.

Rogers, Donald J. *Since You Went Away*. Arlington House, 1973.

Roscoe, Theodore. *United States Submarine Operations in World War II*. Naval Institute Press, 1959.

Ross, Donald K. *"0755" The Heroes of Pearl Harbor*. Rokalu Press, 1988.

Slackman, Michael. *Remembering Pearl Harbor: The Story of the Arizona Memorial*. Honolulu: Arizona Memorial Museum Association, 1992.

_____. *Target: Pearl Harbor*. Honolulu: University of Hawaii Press and Arizona Memorial Museum Association, 1990.

Stillwell, Paul. *Air Raid: Pearl Harbor!* Naval Institute Press, 1981.

_____. *Battleship Arizona*. Naval Institute Press, 1991.

Wallin, Vice Admiral Homer N., USN. *Pearl Harbor: Why, How, Fleet Salvage and Final Appraisal*. U.S. Government Printing Office, 1968.

Wisniewski, Richard A. *Hawaii: The Territorial Years 1900-1959*. Pacific Basin Enterprises, 1989.

Unpublished Sources

National Archives. Various Ships Logs and Action Reports.

Varrill, Robert A. *The White Book of Pearl Harbor Data*.